to Aiden
Happy Birth Day

from Xander

MEDITERRANEO EDITIONS

Greek Mythology

Text by
STELLA KALOGERAKI
Archaeologist

Layout
VANGELIS PAPIOMYTOGLOU

DTP
NATASSA ANTONAKI

Translation
JILL PITTINGER

Sketch
STELLA KALOGERAKI

Copyright 2005
MEDITERRANEO EDITIONS
Tel. +3028310 21590, Fax: +3028310 21591

www.mediterraneo.gr

ISBN: 960-8227-30-5

Greek
Mythology

CONTENTS

The genealogy of the gods

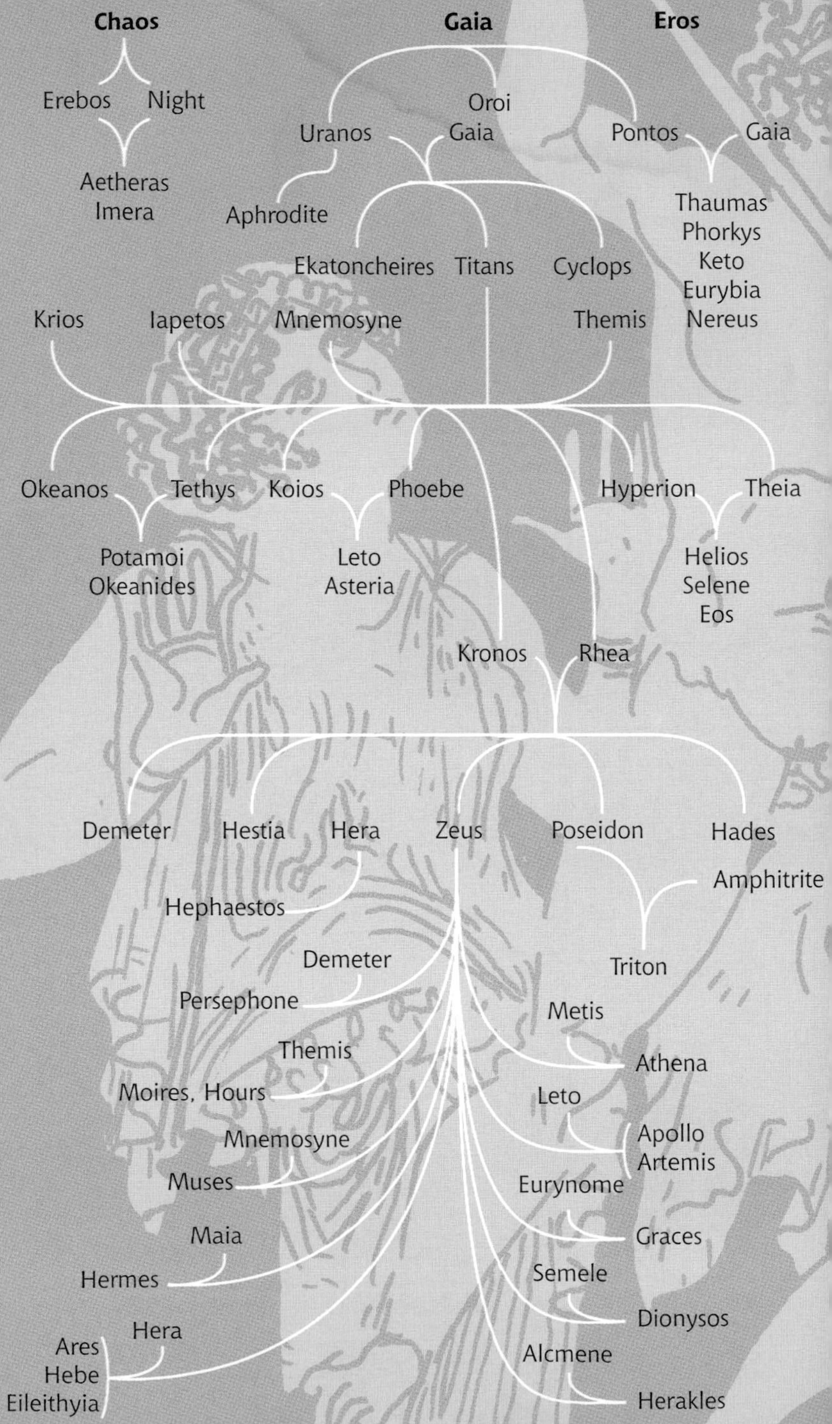

Chaos   **Gaia**   **Eros**

Erebos   Night

Oroi
Gaia

Uranos   Pontos   Gaia

Aetheras
Imera

Aphrodite

Thaumas
Phorkys
Keto
Eurybia
Nereus

Ekatoncheires   Titans   Cyclops

Krios   Iapetos   Mnemosyne   Themis

Okeanos   Tethys   Koios   Phoebe   Hyperion   Theia

Potamoi
Okeanides

Leto
Asteria

Helios
Selene
Eos

Kronos   Rhea

Demeter   Hestia   Hera   Zeus   Poseidon   Hades

Amphitrite

Hephaestos

Demeter

Persephone

Triton

Themis

Metis

Moires, Hours

Athena

Mnemosyne

Leto

Muses

Apollo
Artemis

Maia

Eurynome

Hermes

Graces

Semele

Ares   Hera
Hebe
Eileithyia

Dionysos

Alcmene

Herakles

THEOGONY

Around 700 B.C, the poet Hesiod - a farmer from Boeotia - wrote the "Theogony", which is the most comprehensive work on the creation of the world and the genesis of the gods. According to his account, the first to be created were Chaos, Earth (Gaia), and Love (Erotas). Chaos produced Erebos and Night which in turn gave birth to Aethera, Day (Imera) and Celestial light. Earth produced Sky (Uranos), the mountains, and the sea (Pontos).

After the Earth had given birth to the Sky, the two united to give birth to the twelve Titans, of which six were boys (Okeanos, Iapetos, Koios, Krios, Hyperion and Kronos) and six girls (Rhea, Theia, Mnemonsyne, Themis, Phoebe, Tethys), the Cyclops Brontesi, Steropes, and Arges, and the Hundred Armed Ones - Kottos, Briareos and Gyges, each of whom had one hundred eyes and fifty heads. Since Uranos feared that when his children grew up they would take his throne from him, he locked them away in the depths of the Earth. His wife, however, was unable to accept this state of affairs, and plotted with Kronos, the youngest of the Titans, with the result that while Uranos lay locked in carefree embrace with the Earth, his own son cut off his genitals. From the blood which spouted forth were born the Giants, the Furies and the Meliai - nymphs of the ash trees - while Aphrodite was born from the genitals which were thrown into the sea. Kronos subsequently took power, freeing his brothers and sisters; he imprisoned the Cyclopes and the Hundred Armed Ones, and married his sister Rhea. According to Hesiod, however, Kronos was not the only one to marry one of his own sisters; Okeanos united with

Rhea deceives Kronos by giving him a stone wrapped in swaddling to swallow, instead of Zeus.

Whenever Zeus cried, the Curetes concealed the noise by beating strongly on their shields.

Tethys and produced the rivers and the Okeanides, and Theia and Koios produced Leto and Asteria. Kronos and Rhea produced the three great goddesses Hera, Demeter and Hestia and the three gods Zeus, Poseidon and Hades. Since however Kronos had learned from his parents Uranos and Gaia that one of his offspring would seize power from him, he decided to gobble them up one by one as they were born. Rhea, who like her mother had become very displeased with Kronos' behaviour, wanted to trick him and thus, when she had brought her last child, Zeus, into the world, hid him on Mount Ida in Crete and gave Kronos a stone to swallow instead. After Zeus had been raised under the care of the Nymphs, Amaltheia and the Curetes, he dethroned his father and forced him to vomit up his brothers and sisters. Thereafter, following the pattern of the previous generation, he married his sister Hera. As for his father's power, he shared it with his brothers as follows: he himself became lord of the universe, Poseidon became lord of the sea, and Hades lord of the Underworld.

The Curetes on a shield from the Idaian Cave on Crete

War of the Titans

After having established his power Zeus, with the support of his brothers and sisters who nurtured a terrible hatred for Kronos, decided to wage war on their own father and the Titans, his own brothers and sisters. In the struggle which ensued, Zeus and his siblings had their base on Olympos and the Titans their base on Mount Othrys. Ten whole years passed and the war did not seem to be approaching its end; Gaia now advised Zeus that in order to be victorious he would have to bring on his side his uncles, the **Cyclopes** and the **Hundred Armed Ones**, who were still imprisoned by Kronos in the depths of the

earth. He did this and the Cyclopes, now free, gave Zeus thunderbolts, consisting of lightning and thunder, while the Hundred Armed Ones with all their three hundred arms together raised up huge boulders and crushed the Titans. The Titans were defeated by the terrible barrage of rocks and the thunderbolts of Zeus, and hurled into Tartaros.

"The Farnese Atlas", 2nd century B.C.

Atlas, who was the son of the Titan Iapetos, was condemned by Zeus to hold up the earth and the sky on his shoulders forever. One of the reasons for this punishment was that Atlas, like his brother Prometheus, had disputed the power of Zeus and fought on the side of the Titans.

Zeus fighting a Titan. From the pediment of the Temple of Artemis on Kerkyra (Corfu), c. 590 B.C.

The war of the giants (Gigantomachy). Altar of Zeus at Pergamon, 180 B.C.

War of the Giants

The **Giants**, who were born out of the blood from the mutilation of Uranos by Kronos, were huge, wild anthropomorphic beings which resembled twin snakes from the midriff downwards. At the instigation of

Apollo killed the giant Ephialtes with his sword.

Gaia herself, who had become angry at the harsh behaviour of the gods towards the Titans, the terrible monsters with snakes in their hair and beards began madly to hurl rocks and tree trunks at the Olympians. The

Poseidon pursued the giant Polybotes and crushed him with a piece of the earth which he cut with his trident from the island of Kos. The island of Nisyros was said to have been formed in this way.

Zeus turns the thunder and lightning against the giant Porphyrion and on the right Athena raises her spear and shield against the giant Enkelados, whom she is said to have pursued above the Mediterranean and crushed with a huge rock, which became the island of Sicily.

so that he himself could find the magic plant first. And so it was – as soon as he found it, the opponents began to fall, one by one.

children of Zeus – Athena, Apollo, Hephaestos, and the mortal Herakles – took part in the war which followed, in addition to the great gods themselves. In her endeavour to help the Giants as much as she could, Gaia tried to find a miraculous herb which would ensure them victory. To stop her, Zeus forbade the Sun, the Moon and the Dawn from appearing,

When Zeus defeated the Giants, Gaia was so furious that to obtain her revenge she lay with Tartaros and gave birth to **Typhon** or **Typhoon.** He was the most terrifying and strongest of all her children. From the midriff upwards he was human, but below it he was a dragon; the heads of snakes sprouted from his shoulders and his spittle emitted flames. He was so large that his height reached to the sky; when he held open his arms, one reached to the east and another the west. His appearance cast terror amongst the gods, who changed into animals and hid in Egypt. However, Zeus remained and confronted him. Even though the battle was hard Zeus, with the aid of Athena and Hermes, succeeded in tossing the whole of Etna on top of him, thus crushing him.

THE GENESIS OF MAN

*The two sons of the Titan Iapetos, **Atlas** and **Prometheus**, punished by Zeus for their impiety. The former holds up the earth on his shoulders and the latter lives out the daily torment of an eagle devouring his liver.*

As in the case of most peoples, there was also a belief amongst the Hellenes that the first men were formed from clay: the gods made mortals from earth and fire and subsequently charged Prometheus and Epimetheus, sons of the Titan Iapetos, with their embellishment. The work was undertaken by Epimetheus, who gave strength to some animals, to others speed, and to yet others, dense fur, thick skin, hoofs, or nails; however, since the distribution of the latter characteristics had been indiscriminate and there had been no particular sense behind it, in the end nothing remained for man. When Prometheus came to examine the distribution, he was startled by the nakedness and rudeness of man and decided to help him. Thus he went to Hephaestos, stole fire and gave it to men, teaching them how to use it. Zeus was furious at the impiety

The theft of fire by Prometheus provoked such anger in Zeus that he also wanted to punish men, since they had accepted the gift. **He therefore charged Hephaestos to make a woman out of earth and water and then called upon the goddesses to furnish her with gifts. He sent this woman, whom he called Pandora, to Epimetheus along with a clay jar which was to remain closed forever.** *Epimetheus married Pandora and they lived happily until the time came when she desired to open the jar. Then all calamities flew out of it: war, diseases, death, unhappiness. Even though the inquisitive woman hastened to stopper this source of all tribulations, all that remained inside was hope. We observe thus that with this myth, Hesiod presents Woman as retribution and the source of tribulations in the world.*

of Prometheus and wanted to punish him. He bound him to a stake in the Caucasus, and every morning an eagle came to gnaw at his liver. This torture lasted for thirty years, until Herakles arrived and freed him. According to some sources Prometheus was not only a benefactor of men, but also their very creator – not only because he was the father of Deucalion, but because they believed that he fashioned the first man with his own hands.

*When Prometheus stole the fire from the workshop of Hephaestos, in order to carry it away he hid it inside a giant fennel plant (**Ferula communis**). The shoot of this plant has the property of being able to burn inside without the outer skin being affected.*

Deucalion, son of Prometheus, married his cousin Pyrrha, daughter of Epimetheus and Pandora. According to one myth, when Zeus decided to wipe out the brazen race to which they belonged with a cataclysm, Prometheus advised his son to build an ark and take shelter in it with his wife. Thus they were saved, and when they left the ark, gave thanks to Zeus with a sacrifice. When he asked them what they desired, they asked him for men. Then they began to walk, throwing stones behind them. Men were born from the stones thrown by Deucalion and women from those thrown by Pyrrha. In this way the ancestors of the new human race were born and from these were descended the Hellenes. According to one tradition, their first-born son was named Hellen.

Sarcophagus, 270 B.C. Rome, Capitoline Museum.

The five human races of Hesiod

According to Hesiod, the gods created five races, each following on the destruction of another. First of all there was the race of the Golden Age, which was blessed and existed in happiness. This was followed by the Silver Age; because it was without intelligence and did not revere the gods, it provoked the anger of Zeus who wiped it out and replaced it with the race of the Brazen Age. This race, however, was no better; it invented weapons and war, and was thus destroyed. The fourth race was that of the Heroic Age, to which belonged the heroes of the Trojan War and those of Thebes who lived for eternity in the Islands of the Blest. The final race, that of the Age of Iron, to which Hesiod himself belonged, was condemned because of impiety and corruption to exist amidst torments and worries.

THE GODS

THE GREAT GODS

Zeus
Hera
Athena
Poseidon
Demeter
Apollo
Artemis
Hermes
Aphrodite
Ares
Hephaestos
Dionysos

LESSER GODS AND GROUPS OF DEITIES

GROUPS OF DIVINITIES

THE GREAT GODS

Zeus, Jean-Auguste-Dominique Ingres, 1811, Musée Granet, Aix-en-Provence.

Zeus

The ruler of the world

Father of the gods and men, ruler in the divine palace of Olympos, **Zeus** was the god of the weather, thunder and storms. The root div- of his name, which is met in similar form in the language of other Indo-European peoples, as in the Dyaus pitar of the Indus people and the Roman Diespiter/Jupiter, is related etymologically with the sky and the day (dies). Thus to the father of Heaven and one responsible for changes in the weather, Homer gave a number of epithets, such as 'the cloud mover', 'black-clouded', and 'thundering'. At the same time, in the vernacular the expression 'Zeus is raining' instead of 'it is raining' prevailed. Appropriately, his symbol/weapon was the thunderbolt, which instilled terror and awe in gods and men alike. For this reason, men founded a sanctuary in

his honour wherever the divine lightning struck. Apart from the thunderbolt, which is depicted in the form of a lily, another symbol of Zeus was the eagle, as a fierce, threatening bird which lives in the high mountains. In addition to his connection with the weather, Zeus is associated with the protection of the home (the epithet 'Erkeios' derives from 'erkos' = barrier), property (as indicated by the epithet 'Ktisios'), and guests ('Xenios'). Supremacy and power were not given as a gift to Zeus; he acquired them through a fierce conflict with the Titans, according to the account given by Hesiod in his Theogony. As we have already said Kronos, father of Zeus, was lord of the universe; he swallowed his offspring in the fear that one of them might seize power from him. Zeus was saved thanks to his mother Rhea who, immediately he was born, offered her husband a rock

An oak tree. This sturdiest of trees was dedicated to the mightiest of all the gods.

wrapped in swaddling instead of the child. The infant was reared in the Sacred Cave of Nida, on the mountain called Psiloritis on Crete, with the help of the nymphs, Amaltheia, and the Curetes, who used to dance and bang on their shields in order to conceal the infant's wailing. The fierce war of the Titans, which began as soon as Zeus had grown up, secured his power in the world. His uncles, the Titans, were defeated by their own nephews and nieces, the gods which Kronos had swallowed and Zeus had brought back to life. His battle with the giants and with Typhon (or Typhoon) ended equally in success. As we shall see later, the fear of losing his power to the progeny also afflicted Zeus and led to his systematic and methodic destruction of them. Thus, when **Metis** the wise became pregnant, he swallowed her and there followed the well-known and rather singular birth of Athena from his head. For the same reason he avoided a union with **Thetis** who subsequently married **Peleus** and produced **Achilles**. In this way Thus, he forestalled and eradicated all claimants to the throne, making his power definitive and irrevocable. Strong and more at peace now, he proceeded to marry his sister Hera, while his numerous philanderings with immortals and mortals alike provided him with countless children and determined him as Father of the Gods and of Men.

Victory, Hera, and Zeus. Eastern frieze of the Parthenon, c. 438-432 B.C.

Zeus, Hera and the rest

The official wife of Zeus was his elder sister, **Hera**. According to one tradition the marriage was celebrated on the highest peak of the Ida mountain chain in Asia Minor, after Hera had first seduced Zeus. Others say that the marriage was clearly celebrated with the participation of the gods. Among the wedding gifts was that of Gaia, which consisted of golden apples, known as the Apples of Hesperides. There are many locations where it is claimed that the sacred marriage took place, including Samos and

Boeotia. With his lawful wife Zeus produced Ares, Hebe (later to be the wife of Herakles) and Eileithyia (goddess of childbirth). As for Hephaestos, some say that Hera conceived him by herself, without a man, and others say that he was the son of Zeus. Family life was not something that really mattered to

*With the nymph **Aegina**, daughter of the river Asopos, Zeus fathered Aiakos, who founded the Aiakides amongst whom were the heroes Peleus, Achilles, Neoptolemos and Ajax.*

17

the king of the gods, although he was very attached to his wife. He spent his time chasing goddesses and mortal women and filling the world with children. His inexhaustible amorous activity, which was certainly related to the need for consolidation of the divine genealogical tree and development of the fabric of the myths, provoked the anger of Hera, pushing her to strong outbursts of jealousy. In describing the amorous adventures of Zeus, we follow the reactions of his lawful wife who devised countless plans and passionately pursued her rivals. Zeus was called 'Father of the gods and men', since some of his numerous children belonged to the race of the immortals, others to the race of mortals, depending on each consort he chose. With Metis, the daughter of Okeanos and Tethys and the goddess who had gathered all wisdom in her head, Zeus fathered Pallas Athena, goddess of wisdom. The singular birth of the fully armed Athena from the head of her father derives from the fact that Zeus, fearing that he would lose his power through the offspring of Metis, swallowed her whole while she was still pregnant. The same fear prevented him from a union with Thetis; despite his great passion for her, he married her to Peleus. Asteria and Leto were the daughters of the Titans, Koios and Phoebe. Zeus pursued Asteria who, in order to escape, changed first into a quail and then into a wandering, rocky island which was named Ortygia (island of the quails). After Asteria he pursued Leto and united with her in Miletus on the coast of Asia Minor. When the time came for her to give birth, she was pursued by Hera and could find no place for the lying-in. After much roving her sister took her in and thus Apollo and Artemis were born on Ortygia, which thereafter ceased to be a wandering island, but appeared in the world and took the name of Delos. Zeus lay with Maia, one of the daughters of Atlas, in Kyllene and fathered

*According to one account he transformed himself into a swan and lay with **Leda**, wife of Tyndareus king of Sparta, and fathered Helen, the future wife of Menelaos who was responsible for the Trojan War, as well as the Dioscurides ('the sons of Zeus') Castor and Pollux. There is an alternative version to this story; Zeus was seized with passion for one of the daughters of Night, winged Nemesis whose name means retribution. Angered at his pursuit of her, she began to transform herself so that he would not find her. First she became a fish, then a goose. Zeus transformed himself into a swan and coupled with the goose, which produced an egg. Leda found the egg and took it with her, and Helen subsequently emerged from the egg. Leonardo da Vinci, 1510-15, Gallery Borghese, Rome*

Hermes, messenger of the gods. In addition to his marriage with Hera, Zeus united with his second sister, Demeter, and fathered Persephone who later became the wife of Hades. The ill-fated Semele, daughter of King Kadmos, was burned by the thunderbolt of her own lover, Zeus, through intervention by Hera. Since she was already carrying Dionysos, according to one account, Zeus took the child from womb of the dead woman and sewed him into his thigh until the time came for his birth. With Themis, the daughter of

Although there are countless stories of both deities and mortals who aroused the passion of Zeus, not even men escaped his amorous interests. Thus according to one story, after having changed into an eagle he snatched **Ganymede** from Troy, and brought him to Olympos where he made him cup-bearer to the gods.

In Argos, he managed to unite with **Danäe**, whose father had kept her locked up so that she would not bear a child which would seize power from him; Zeus entered her cell in the form of a golden shower. Thus, Perseus was born.

Uranos and Gaia who was thus his aunt and may have been his first wife, he fathered the Hours (Eunomia, Dike, and Irene) and the Fates (Klotho, Lachesis, and Atropos). While Themis, according to the etymology of her name, represented the laws of nature, the Fates on the one hand were connected with the laws of life, but the Hours with the suitability of the moment in time, and ripeness. However, the union of Zeus with his other aunt, Mnemonsyne who was also a daughter of sky and earth, produced the nine Muses, who lived on Olympos and bestowed joy and serenity upon gods

and men. The sea nymph Eurynome, daughter of Okeanos and Tethys, bore him the three Graces - Aglaia, Euphrosyne and Thaleia. Apart from his predilection for goddesses and nymphs, Zeus often desired mortal women and in order to possess them would frequently resort to the method of metamorphosis. He also lay with Niobe and Io in Argos. With the former he fathered Argos and Pelasgos and with the latter, Epaphos. He lay with the nymph Callisto in Arkadia and thus Arkas was born, the progenitor of the

Arkadians. In order to possess another mortal woman, Alcmene of Thebes, Zeus took on the shape of her husband, Amphitryon. As Alcmene also lay with her husband on the following day, twins were born – Herakles was fathered by Zeus and Iphicles by Amphitryon.

One of the better-known stories is that concerning **Europa**, daughter of king Agenor and Telephassa. While this royal girl was gathering flowers, he appeared to her in the shape of a **bull**, tricked her and carried her off to Crete, where he lay with her and fathered three sons, Minos, Rhadamanthos and Sarpedon.

Hera

Immortal wife

Hera, daughter of Kronos and Rhea, was chosen by her brother to be his lawful and immortal wife. Her name is probably connected with the word 'ora', which means 'suitable time', or 'ripeness'. Hera is the embodiment of a woman who is fertile and ripe for marriage. The main places where she was worshipped were Samos, at the famous Heraion, which was a magnificent temple dedicated to

her, and Argos, from which she took the epithet 'Argeía'. As the protectoress of marriage, for which function she was known as 'Gamostólos', that is, the one who prepares a marriage, and 'Teleía', meaning 'perfect', she was worshipped in many more places in Greece, such as Olympia, Tiryns, and Lesbos, and also in Southern Italy. Despite the fact that she symbolizes womanhood and the wife, her connection with motherhood is limited. Although she had four children, the only remarkable one was Ares, the god of war, who was not, however, beloved by his father. Her other two children, Hebe and Eileithyia were secondary entities in the mythological kingdom, while in the case of Hephaestos it is said that she bore him herself, without Zeus. Her character

was far removed from that of a good mother and instead is very harsh with her children, especially with Hephaestos, and

vindictive with the children of Zeus. Her problematic relationship with the ruler of the universe is said to have begun long before the marriage, when a secret amorous relationship existed between brother and sister. Hera, however, who had managed every year to renew her virginity by bathing in the spring of Kanathos near Nauplion, entered the married state on Samos, which was called

*With its great many red seeds, the pomegranate **(Punica granatum)** symbolized fertility and for this reason was sacred to Hera, goddess of marriage and the family. The fruit is also connected with the myth of the abduction of Persephone by Hades, and with the two great goddesses Athena and Aphrodite.*

21

'Parthenia', and she herself was worshipped as 'Parthénos' – the virgin. It is said that her first union with Zeus took place on Mount Thornax. When the goddess had gone to walk there, Zeus had summoned up a downpour and changed himself into a cuckoo, which fell at her feet, trembling from the cold. As soon as Hera took the bird into her arms to warm it, Zeus regained his true form and lay with her. From that time on the mountain was called Kokkygas, meaning cuckoo.

The story concerning Hephaestos is indicative of the character of Hera. When she gave birth to him, because he was ugly and lame, she threw him into the sea. To his good fortune, the Okeanides Thetis and Eurynome gathered him up and raised him in secret. At some stage, however, he became bored in the sea kingdom and decided to go to Olympos, his natural home as the son of Zeus and Hera. He constructed a golden throne and sent it as a gift to his mother. When she in her delight sat on the throne to try it out, she found herself suddenly bound with invisible nets. In exchange for freeing her, he took Aphrodite as his wife and was thus accepted on Olympos.

The jealous one, the vengeful, the pitiless

The ever-deceived wife sought to be cleansed from the insults to her, taking revenge against her husband on the one hand, and against her rivals on the other. Scores of episodes describe her wild interventions, her tough stance and her machinations against the mistresses of her husband and their offspring. Blinded by jealousy she prevented Leto from giving birth, forcing her to wander from place to place at the hour of her lying-in. She not only changed Io into a cow but also sent a gadfly to sting her. While Semele was pregnant with Dionysos, she imbued her with a consuming desire to see Zeus in all his majesty and thus she was burned alive by his brilliance; she changed Kallisto, the mother of Arkas, into a bear and made Artemis herself kill the animal. Apart from her behaviour towards Zeus' lovers, she madly pursued her children. Thus, we observe her persecution of Herakles from the first moment of his birth, sending snakes to his cradle and later making him the slave of Eurystheus, king of Mycenae. Her madness is so great that it leads her to undermine her own husband and to bring about the dissolution of her family. She takes the side of the Trojans in the Trojan War and finally decides to separate. However, her attempt to regain her lost dignity by abandoning Zeus comes to nothing. When he indicates that he is going to remarry and decks out a bride made of wood, Hera loses her composure once more, falls upon the "bride" and rips the clothes to shreds; thus she is once more a victim of one of Zeus' farces.

Hera and Herakles

22

Athena

The wise daughter and her strange birth

The sea nymph Metis, daughter of Oceanos and Tethys, became pregnant by her cousin Zeus. As she was the embodiment of wisdom and discretion, there was no doubt that she would bear equally clever children. It was said that she would have a daughter first and then a son who would seize power from Zeus. The latter, fearing that his position would be upset, deceived the pregnant nymph and swallowed her. Thus,

"Athena musing", c. 460 B.C. Acropolis Museum, Athens.

a little while later on the banks of the river Triton, he himself gave birth to the child which Metis had carried; this child was the most wise maiden, the goddess Athena who for this reason was called 'Tritogenia'. Her birth took place in a very strange and at the same time remarkable manner.

According to Hesiod, Athena sprang from the head of Zeus. It is said too that Hephaestos (or Prometheus) was the one who opened the head of his father with an axe so that the fully armed maiden sprang out, emitting war cries.

Maiden and warrior but not enamoured of war

The goddess Athena, whose temple known as the Parthenon dominates Athens, seems to have taken her name from the city, although some believe that it was exactly the opposite. Already, on Linear B tablets from Knossos there is mention of 'atana potinija', meaning 'gracious one/lady of Athens', evidence which leads to the conclusion that the place-name already existed. Certainly, in accordance with the legend, Athena won the

*Although a warlike goddess – '**Athena Promachos**' – she often came into conflict with the war god par excellence, Ares. Their contests, which are frequently hand-to-hand on the field of battle, indicate concepts of war which are completely different from one another. The one (Ares) revels in war and thirsts for blood, while the other (Athena) is the calm advocate of methodical strategy. Their clash, therefore, represents the contrast between physical and intellectual superiority. While it appears that we have two warlike deities, in reality only Ares belongs to this category while Athena is elevated to the goddess of wisdom.*

The Parthenon (built 447-432 B.C.)

battle with Poseidon, giving her name to the city. The epithet 'Pallas' means 'one who brandishes weapons', or 'young girl'. Athena is the exact embodiment of the armed maiden, incorruptible and invincible. She is present on the field of battle, moving around and imparting vigour to the Achaeans, whose side she took in the Trojan War. She chose to protect certain individuals, among them Achilles, Herakles, Odysseus and Telemachos. Her birth from the head of her father indicates her very close connection with him, and it is evident that Zeus singled her out from among all his offspring. This is why he bestowed upon her his aegis, the breastplate from the skin of the goat Amaltheia which had become his insignia. Later on, when Athena helped Perseus to cut off the head of the Gorgon Medusa, he presented the head to her and Athena placed it in the centre of the aegis in order to turn to stone [gorgonise] whoever dared to gaze upon it. Others said that the breastplate of Athena was the skin of Pallas which the goddess acquired when she flayed the giant during the War of the Giants, and believed thus that the epithet Pallas derives from his name. Athena supported her father in the battle against the Giants; she helped Herakles destroy Alkyonos, flayed Pallas, pursued Enkelados and crushed him beneath the island of Sicily, and she brought about the beheading of the Gorgon Medusa who had allied herself with the Giants.

Athenian tetradrachm, 449-413 B.C.

Fighter and housewife, maiden and mother

During periods of peace, when Athena did not have to work out strategies, she was concerned with the promotion of culture and technology. Her work and obligations did not stop on the battle front; immediately after a war was over, she returned to her peaceful state in order to begin new duties: the improvement of everyday life with the development of art and technology. She taught men how to cultivate the olive, how to weave, how to construct ships, how to build, and how to make weapons and tools. As Athena 'Ergána' she taught the first woman, Pandora, how to use a loom. In her battle with Poseidon over who would become protector of Athens, she planted the first olive tree on the Acropolis, and was thus chosen as patroness of Athens (Athena Poliás). In addition she contributed to the perfection of weapons, as evidenced by her shield, breastplate and spear; it is also said that she invented the flute and the first statues.

While both a housekeeper and mistress of the house, Athena never became a wife. She remained 'the maiden' in spite of the fact that she became a mother and was venerated as one. The story connected with this is as follows: Hephaestos, who assisted at her birth, wanted to possess her. She however, refused and from his seed, which fell onto the earth, **Erichthonios** or **Erichtheus**, first king of Athens, was born. Athena took an interest in the child and put him in a basket; she then gave it to the three daughters of Cecrops who looked after it on the understanding that they would not open it. Aglauros, however, together with one of her sisters, opened the basket out of curiosity. It is said that they were driven mad by what they saw and hurled themselves from the Acropolis rock.

Poseidon

"The Poseidon of Artemision", c. 460 B.C. National Archaeological Museum, Athens.

Lord of the earthquakes and shipwrecks

Poseidon was the son of Kronos and Rhea and the brother of Zeus. Although his name, according to one source, means 'lord/ husband of the earth' he was the lord of the seas and of the waters in general. With regard to the apportioning of the world Homer recorded that Kronos divided it amongst his sons as follows: Zeus took the sky, Poseidon the sea and Hades the underworld. It is also mentioned in the Iliad that the earth and Olympos belonged to all three together. The characteristic hallmark, symbol and weapon of Poseidon was the trident and he was considered the protector of fisherman, who always venerated him as the storm was considered to be his exclusive area of responsibility. In addition to the palace on Olympos which he shared with the other gods, he also maintained one of his own, his private palace located at Aeges in the depths of the Aegean Sea; there he lived with his wife Amphitrite. Although lord of the sea, he is particularly associated with the earth and considered to be god of the earthquake and generally responsible for other geological phenomena. Thus he was worshipped as 'Asphaleion', that is to say 'responsible for stability' and, as Xenophon indicates, at time of earthquake men raised the paean to Poseidon. As 'Petraios' and 'Hippios', he is connected with the horse, which is the

The Temple of Poseidon at Sounion, built 450-440 B.C.

animal sacred to him. There was a belief amongst some that he was the father of the horse which was born one night when he poured out his seed onto a

Although he was lord of the seas and the father of the horse, the invention of the ship, and of reins and the bridle was ascribed to Athena. Perhaps this was a way to

underline the conflict between them, which culminated in the contest for supremacy in Athens. Despite his greater age and his austere and threatening character,

rock; others said that he impregnated the Gorgon Medusa and, when Perseus beheaded her, Pegasos and a fully armed warrior, Chrysaor, sprang from her head. Still others believed that he lay with his sister Demeter and the horse named Areion was born.

*It was also said in the case of **Theseus**, the great hero and king of Athens, that he was a son of **Poseidon** by **Aethra**. According to the myth Athena herself devised the union of the god with Aethra shortly before the marriage of the latter to king Aegeus. According to one account Aegeus, who drowned in the sea and gave his name to it, continued his life in the watery kingdom, and was the hypostasis for Poseidon himself.*

his position is shown to be inferior to that of his niece who rules Athens, tames the horse and in some way exercised power in the sea. These juxtapositions make clear the symbolism of superiority of the mind and technical ability over strong natural powers, even including those of the earthquake and tempest.

Triton

Productive love affairs

Like his brother Zeus, Poseidon also had many amorous adventures and fathered countless children. According to one account, when Poseidon was born Rhea, in order to protect him from his father Kronos, took him to Rhodes and left him there with the natives of the island, the Telchines. As excellent, well-known craftsmen they made him his trident. When the god reached adulthood, he fell in love with one of the Telchines' sisters, Alia, and produced six sons and one daughter with her. The daughter was called Rhodos and the island took its name from her. The sons were said to have been very fierce and, when they prevented Aphrodite from stopping on the island on her way from Kythera to Cyprus, she sent them madness and instilled in them a passion for their own mother. Poseidon, in order to punish them, sank them into the depths of the earth, while Alia fell into the sea and from then on was called Lefkothea. The official wife of Poseidon was the Nereid Amphitrite, daughter of Nereus and Doris. With her he fathered Triton, a sea deity who was a man from the midriff upwards while the rest of him was a fish. According to one view, this sea spirit ruled in the waters long before Poseidon did. Like his son, he was concerned with the care of his sea chariot and with filling the sea with beautiful sound by blowing into seashells. With Iphimedeia, wife of Aloeus, Poseidon fathered two terrible giants, Otos and Ephialtes. It was said that Iphimedeia was so enamoured of Poseidon that she dived into the sea every day in order to remain pregnant by the god of the waters, until Poseidon appeared before her in the form of the river Enipeus and united with her. The giant Tityos was also considered to be a son of Poseidon by Elára,

*The giant **Orion** was a son of Poseidon by Euryale, the daughter of Minos, and is said to have received the gift of being able to walk on the waves from his father. One of many legends says that he spent the final years of his life on Crete, hunting with Artemis and Leto. Since he was such a very good hunter Gaia was afraid that all beasts would disappear, so she sent a scorpion to give him a deadly bite. Then Artemis asked her father to honour him and Zeus changed Orion into a constellation.*

daughter of Orchomenos. It is said that when, urged on by Hera, he tried to rape Leto and her daughter Artemis, he was struck dead by a thunderbolt from Zeus. The winged horse Pegasos and Chrysaor who sprang from the head of the gorgon Medusa when it was struck off, were also children of Poseidon. Similarly, there was the divine horse Areion, to which Demeter gave birth when she changed into a mare in order to escape the amorous pursuit of her brother. Even the goddess of beauty, Aphrodite, did not escape his attentions and thus bore Erykas who ruled in Sicily. It was also said that Busiris, king of Egypt, was a son of Poseidon by Lysianassa, daughter of Epaphos. With Libya he had a son, the invincible giant Antaios who made all those who passed through his country fight with him. As well as Antaios, many other sons of Poseidon found themselves in a difficult position with Herakles, with whom the god did not have good relations. Amykos, his child by a nymph, was king of the Vervyki, in the region of the Bosporus; he also provoked passers-by into a boxing match, but was defeated by the Argonauts. His son Alirrothios by

Poseidon *is connected with Crete through the myth of the* ***Minotaur***. *When Minos wanted to become king he asked Poseidon to give him a sign in order to certify his acceptance. The god sent a beautiful bull from the waves. Minos was satisfied, but he neglected to sacrifice the animal to the god. Poseidon was angry, and in order to punish the ungracious king, imbued his wife, Pasiphäe, with a passion for the beautiful animal. Queen and bull coupled and thus the Minotaur was born, a terrible monster with the body of a man and the head of a bull which fed on human blood. The Minotaur was defeated much later by Theseus, who according to one account was the son of Poseidon. Giulio Romano (1492-1546), Palazzo del Te, Mantua.*

the nymph Evryti raped Alcippe, daughter of Ares, but was killed by the king of war himself. The thief Procrustes was also believed to be a son of Poseidon; the hero Theseus killed him in his own bed. Finally, the one-eyed Cyclops, Polyphemos, who was blinded by Odysseus, was a son of Poseidon by Thoousa.

Bellerophon*, son of Poseidon and Eurymede, riding on Pegasus, the winged horse which was also the offspring of Poseidon by Medusa.*

Demeter

Demeter, Triptolemos, and Persephone, 440-430 B.C. National Archaeological Museum, Athens.

Persephone, being designated together as 'Mother and Daughter' or 'Demeter and Daughter', and also as 'the Two Goddesses'. Persephone, snatched away by Hades who made her his wife, became a goddess and the Lady of the Underworld. Thus the close connection of Mother and Daughter is underlined by the immediate relationship and by the 'adjacency' of the areas over which they ruled – one was the goddess of the crops, and the other goddess of the underworld beneath them. They were worshipped together at many festivals which were nearly all related to the cultivation of the soil; for example, the Thalysia was held in December in order to bless the green and verdant growth and taste the new wine, then there was the Skyrofória, the Thesmofória associated with the autumn seed-time etc.

Demeter was the daughter of Kronos and Rhea and the sister of Zeus, Hera, Poseidon, Hades and Hestia. Her name means 'mother of the earth' and most probably by extension 'mother of the crops'. Apart from the etymology of the name, there is no doubt that Demeter is associated with crops, as is shown by the prayers and dedications in her honour made by farmers. She is a rustic goddess who was worshipped in the open air with analogous titles of 'karpofóros' (fruitful), and 'Sito' (of the corn). In Cyprus, the verb used to denote the harvesting of the grain was 'damatrízein' which clearly derives from the name of the goddess, Demeter or Damater. She was closely associated with her daughter,

Triptolemos, whose name means 'he who ploughs the field three times', is sometimes referred to as the king of Eleusis along with Keleos, and sometimes as his son. It is believed that he was chosen by Demeter and the Daughter to bestow the cultivation of grain upon the world and that he invented the first plough and was the first to till, sow, reap and thresh in the area of Eleusis. Thereafter he traversed all the inhabited world and gave his knowledge of the cultivation of the earth to mankind.

The kidnapping of Persephone

Hades (Pluto), god of the Underworld, fell in love with Persephone, daughter of Demeter and Zeus, and decided to have her
for himself. However, since he was certain that her mother would
never let her leave her side, he decided to carry her off. One
day, when the young girl was playing with the Okeanides, a
beautiful narcissus appeared in front of her; it had been sent by
Gaia to deceive her. Persephone was captivated by its beauty
and when she went to pick it, the earth opened, her uncle Pluto
emerged in his golden chariot, snatched her and bore her away to
his kingdom. When the young girl cried out for help she was heard only by Hecate, Helios
and her mother; the latter was very distressed and ran to look for her. For nine days the
unhappy Demeter wandered the seas and the land but could not find her. She arrived,
sorrowing, in Eleusis, at the palace of Keleos. There she asked to rest, pretending that
she was from Crete and had arrived there with pirates in pursuit. The daughters of Keleos
felt sorry for her and decided to ask their mother, Metaneira, to engage the old lady as a
nurse for her new-born son. When she entered the chamber of the queen, her head grew
up to touch its ceiling and a divine light spread everywhere. Metaneira greeted her and
entrusted her with her baby. Thus Demophon was raised in the arms of Demeter as a god.
She considered making him immortal and to this end - amongst other things - she placed
him in the fire every evening in order to burn away his mortal aspect. One evening, out
of curiosity, the queen secretly watched the education of her son, provoking the anger of
Demeter. In a rage, she revealed herself and said that Demophon would not now become
an immortal but would receive honour from mortals for eternity. She also demanded
that a temple be built for her. Therein she remained, mourning for her daughter. As
the harvest was very bad in that year Zeus sent winged Iris and all the gods to ask her
to come back. She, in exchange, demanded the return of her daughter and Zeus sent
Hermes to ask Hades to bring Persephone to the upper world. Hades consented, but he
had previously and in secret given his wife a pomegranate seed to eat, so that she would
not remain with her mother forever. Hermes took the Daughter in his chariot and brought
her to the temple of her Mother. Immediately after an enthusiastic and moving greeting
Demeter asked Persephone whether Hades had given her anything to eat. She remember
the pomegranate and then they realized that Persephone was obliged in the future to
stay for one third of the year in the underworld
but could spend the remaining two-thirds with the
other immortals. Mother and Daughter went up
joyfully to Olympos where they were welcomed
by Zeus. Before that, however, he made the fields
blossom forth and taught the kings the mysteries
and the sacred rites in order to worship her and
always have her good favour and a good harvest.

Silver tetradrachm,
c. 310 B.C.
Chicago, Fine Arts
Museum.

The Rape of Persephone,
Albrecht Dürer, 1516.

The sleep-bringing
poppy (**Papaver
somniferum**) was
associated with
Demeter, the goddess
of fruitfulness. It was
said that when Hades
snatched her daughter
from her, she soothed
her pain with the sedative
juice of the flower.

Apollo

The Apollo triad: Leto, Apollo, Artemis

Zeus desired his cousins, Leto and Asteria, daughters of the Titan Koios and Phoebe, and wanted to lay with them. In order to escape from him Asteria changed herself into a quail and Zeus, to pursue her, took the shape of an eagle. Then Asteria turned into a rock and fell into the sea to hide herself. Thus she became a rocky islet called Ortygia, or island of the quails, which was not fixed in one place but floated in the Aegean. After Asteria, Zeus lay with Leto, but when the time came for her to give birth, the anger and jealousy of Hera prohibited any place from taking her in. It was said that she could only give birth in a place which had never seen the sun. Thus began the tragic wanderings throughout Greece of a woman on the point of motherhood. According to an alternative version of the myth, Leto in her hopeless situation asked her sister Asteria, who had become an island, to receive her. Then indeed, the floating rock 'appeared', became anchored in the depths and from then on was called Delos. Her torments, however, had not ended. Even though she had found a place she could not give birth, because Hera had plunged Eileithyia, the goddess of childbirth, into ignorance of her state. For nine days and nights she suffered labour pains, until the great goddesses who had gone to stand by Leto sent Iris, messenger of the gods, to inform Eileithyia secretly and unknown to Hera. So the hour of the birth arrived. Leto, in torment, embraced the palm tree which had grown in front of her, knelt on the ground and the wonder took place'; amidst psalms and hymns Apollo emerged, bathed in light. Barren Delos flowered and shone forth and produced an olive tree with golden leaves. Themis fed the new-born babe with nectar and ambrosia. The new god grew up at great speed and announced that from thenceforth he would concern himself with the bow and the lyre and would proclaim the will of Zeus through oracles. He immediately left the island in his glory and went up to Olympos. All the gods were quite afraid and rose from their seats, except for Zeus and Leto who remained seated.

Statue of **Apollo** from the west pediment of the Temple of Zeus at Olympia, c. 457 B.C. Archaeological Museum of Olympia.

The giant **Tityos**, son of Gaia or of Zeus and Elara, was killed by **Apollo** when he tried to rape Leto, his mother. Others believed that the lightning of Zeus struck him down. They said that Hera had sent the giant in order to have her revenge on the mistress of her husband who had gone to Delphi, the place where her son was worshipped.

The "omphalos" at Delphi. Hellenistic/Roman copy, Museum of Delphi.

Apollo Pythios and Delphinios

In order to make known the will of Zeus and to give prophecies, as he had declared at the hour of his birth Apollo had to establish an oracle. The choice of a location, however, was not easy. After enough wandering he arrived at the waters of Telphousa, which were ruled over by the nymph of the same name. Liking the place, he announced his intentions to the nymph; she however, thinking carefully and concluding that if Apollo came there she would lose her glory and her power, showed him a better place – Krisa, below Parnassos. There, as if the wild location with its huge cliffs were not enough, he had to face a female snake which guarded its only spring, that of Kastalia, and threatened all who drew near. Having aimed his bow at it and killed it with his arrow, he left the snake to rot under the sun, which gave rise to the epithet Pythios, from a word meaning 'to rot'. Others said that the epithet came from the name of the snake, which was Python, and still

Apollo and Daphne. Raphael Regius, Venice, c. 1513.

According to Pausanias, before the oracle of Apollo at Delphi there was an oracle of Poseidon and Gaia, where the latter herself gave prophecies. Later on, Gaia gave it to her daughter Themis and she gave it as a gift to Apollo. The first priestess of the oracle there was Phimonoe. Pausanias writes that the very first temple of Apollo was a shelter made of laurel. The next was constructed by bees from wax and feathers. The third temple was the work of Hephaestos and Athena, wrought from bronze and according to one tradition, destroyed by fire. The fourth temple was of stone, and also destroyed by fire; it was built by Trophonios and Agamides. The architect of the last temple, according again to Pausanias, was someone named Spintharos who came from Corinth.

that they would be his first priests. He changed himself into a dolphin, entered the ship and brought it into the harbour at Krisa. Thence, taking the form of a star, he went to Delphi and returned in the shape of a young man. He presented himself to the Cretans and revealed that he was Apollo. After they had built an altar to him on the shore, which was to be called 'Delphinios', he ordered them to accompany him to the site of the oracle where they would become priests. In a procession, led by the god himself, they were taken to the place others gave the name of the snake, which was female, as Délphina or Délphini. He had his revenge against Telphousa by making her spring disappear and building his altar in the same spot. His next step after the foundation of the oracle at Delphi was to populate it with priests. While he was thinking about this, he noticed a boat containing Cretan merchants who were traveling from Knossos to Pylos, and decided where they were to spend the rest of their lives, and when they saw the rocks and the dryness of the place and complained to the god, he assured them that the offerings and sacrifices made by men there would be so many that they would have no need to practice any type of cultivation or occupation.

The loves of Apollo

Akersekómas Apollo, that is to say the god 'whose hair was uncut', embodied the end of youth and the beginning of adulthood with entry into the community of men. Handsome and dazzling, a true Greek kouros, he could not help but have many passionate and amorous adventures. His solar halo and his extreme beauty were the prerequisites for rich and often dangerous amorous activity with both men and women.

His first love was considered to have been Daphne who, according to one account was a nymph and daughter of the river Peneios, and to another the daughter of king Amyklas. Despite her indescribable beauty Daphne did not want to marry and preferred to hunt in the forests with Artemis. One day, Apollo met

The lyre, and music in general, connected Apollo and the Muses. He lay with two of them – Kalliope and Thaleia – and produced the Korybantes and Orpheus.

the nymph in the countryside and tried to lay with her. She began to run and when she realized that the god was going to catch her, sought help from her father who changed her

*Despite her indescribable beauty **Daphne** did not want to marry and preferred to hunt in the forests with Artemis. One day, Apollo met the nymph in the countryside and tried to lay with her. She began to run and when she realized that the god was going to catch her, sought help from her father who changed her into a tree. From then on the laurel (bay) tree was associated with the worship of Apollo and became his sacred tree. It provided his garland and the Delphic tripod, while the Pythia herself chewed laurel leaves in order to be able to give the prophecies.*

Apart from Asklepios who was a physician, another son of Apollo, this time with Cyrene, was **Aristaios** who saved men from epidemics. It was said that Aristaios, who was taught prophecy and healing by the Muses, was the one who discovered bee-keeping and the process of olive oil production.

story that he was not his son, but that of Magnetas, and Apollo loved him passionately. Apollo could not satisfy his love for the nymph Marpessa because Zeus came between them. According to the myth, Marpessa was in love with Idas. When the two of them fell into the clutches of Zeus he made the nymph choose between them. She chose Idas because she knew that Apollo had eternal beauty and when she herself aged he would abandon her. Apollo lay with Koronis, daughter of king Phlegyas who ruled in Lakereia, a city of Thessaly, and Asklepios was born. At the very moment of the birth of the baby his mother died from the arrows of Artemis. Apollo had set her to kill Koronis because while she was pregnant she had dared to proceed with a marriage with Ischys, son of Elatos. Apollo gave the infant Asklepios to Cheiron to be brought up. Thus he was taught medicine by the Centaur and became an important and renowned

into a tree. From then on the laurel (bay) tree was associated with the worship of Apollo and became his sacred tree. It provided his garland and the Delphic tripod, while the Pythia herself chewed laurel leaves in order to be able to give the prophecies. Those who believe that Daphne was the daughter of a king relate that Leukippos, son of king Oinomaos, had fallen in love with her. In order to get near to her he disguised himself as a girl; Daphne became fond of the 'girl' because of her success in the hunt. This made Apollo jealous and one day he inspired the girls to bathe naked in the river Ladon. Thus the deceit was revealed and they fell upon him and killed him.

From his relations with the Muse Tháleia the fearsome Korybantes were born; they were musicians and dancers, famous for the protection which they had afforded Zeus while he was a child, so that his father Kronos would not hear his wails. In addition to Thaleia he lay with the Muse Kalliópe and fathered Orpheus and Hymen. In the case of the latter there is one physician. However, when he came to the point of raising the dead, Zeus sent a thunderbolt which killed him. Apollo, to exact retribution for the loss of his son, killed the Cyclopes who fashioned the thunderbolts of Zeus. To punish him for this, Zeus made him a shepherd of the mortal kingdom of Admetos, near Pheres in Thessaly. With Mantó, the daughter of the seer Calchas, Apollo produced Mopsos who was himself a seer. It was said that he was so talented that when he disputed with his father he showed himself to be wiser, and then Calchas died of sorrow. In order to possess Cassandra, daughter of Priam and Hecuba, Apollo promised her that he would teach her the art of prophecy. Since however she deceived him, he punished her by taking away her ability to be believed. Thereafter Cassandra could prophecy, but nobody would believe her. Apollo lay with Akálli, the daughter of Minos. They produced three sons: Miletos, Kydon and Naxos. It is said that Apollo raped Créusa, the daughter of the king of Athens. She became pregnant and when she had given birth, abandoned the child, named Ion, who was brought up under the care of the Pythia and later became the king of Athens.

In addition to women, Apollo passionately loved boys. Apart from Hymen, the god fell passionately in love with Hyákinthos, whose mother was the Muse Kleio; his father was Pieros. Apollo killed Hyakinthos by mistake while they were playing at throwing the discus together and from his blood there sprang up the wild flower of the same name. It is clear that the amorous relationships and above all the offspring of Apollo indicate the physiognomy of this god. Thus his connection with prophecy is reinforced through his association with Manto, Mopsos and Cassandra, his connection with music through the Muses, the Korybantes and Orpheus, and his connection with medicine through Asklepios and Aristaios.

In the Trojan War, Apollo fought on the side of the Trojans. Certainly, when Hera, Athena and Poseidon conspired in order to lull Zeus to sleep so that they could defeat the Trojans, Zeus himself sent Apollo with his aegis and overturned their plans. Nevertheless, he honoured the dead king of Lycia, Sarpedon, who had been killed at the hands of Patroclos, by taking care of him and handing him over to his brothers, Hypnos (Sleep) and Thanatos (Death), to bring him back to his own country. The same god set Hector to kill Patroclos and directed the arrow of Paris to the weak part of the body of Achilles, his heel.
Ares, Aphrodite, Leto, Artemis, Apollo And Zeus watching the Trojan War. Eastern frieze of the Treasury of the Siphnians at Delphi, c. 530 B.C.

Artemis and Aktaeon, Raphael Regius, Venice c. 1513.

Artemis

Wild and untamed maiden

Artemis, daughter of Zeus and Leto, was born on exactly the same day and under the same circumstances as Apollo. It was said that she emerged from the womb of Leto first and then helped her mother to give birth to Apollo. Thus twins were born, the boy as the embodiment of the sun and the girl as that of the moon. While still a small child she decided to remain unmarried and asked her father to exempt her from the bonds of marriage. She lived in the mountains and hunted wild animals, dancing and playing in company with young girls who stayed with her until the time came for them to be married.

She was called 'Keladiní', meaning 'unruly' and 'noisy', because she liked bows and arrows, dancing, and shouting. Her impetuousness and liveliness are shown in pictorial representations where she has a short tunic, quiver, and bow and is always accompanied by an animal – a stag or a deer. She was a beautiful maiden with the wildness of a boy. In the Iliad Homer calls her 'Pótnia Therón', meaning 'the Mistress of the Animals' and of Nature in general. The goddess, while the maiden or virgin, is at the same time a goddess of childbirth. Thus 'Locheía' or 'Lechó' Artemis is associated with Eileithyia. The clothes of women who had died in childbirth were placed as an offering in the sanctuary of Artemis at Vravrona.

> **'Sweet Maiden'**
> In Minoan Crete a deity was worshipped with the name of **Britomartis**, which means 'sweet maiden'. It was said that king Minos fell in love with this goddess who had exactly the same attributes as Artemis and was most probably an earlier personification of her. He had seen her hunt in the Cretan forests and tried to lay with her. Running away, she reached a sheer cliff and jumped into the sea. She was caught in the nets of some fishermen and from then on named 'Diktynna'.

*The palm tree of Theophrastus (**Phoenix theophrasti**) is connected with Artemis and Apollo who were born in the shade of its branches on Delos. This palm, which is indigenous to Crete, is said to have been taken to Delos by Theseus when at some stage he organized games in honour of the god on the island.*

Woe to anyone who dared to look at the virgin girls when they were bathing naked in the lakes and rivers! In particular, woe to anyone who in any way insulted Artemis, the ultimate pure and untouchable virgin. **Aktaeon**, son of Aristaios and Autonoe, committed this mistake in his desire to see her naked while she bathed in the streams of Kithairon. She immediately changed him into a stag and set her fifty hounds to tear him apart.

Harsh avenger

On the eve of the Trojan War, in the absence of a wind that would enable the boats to set sail, Agamemnon, brother of Menelaos king of Sparta, went out hunting. By misfortune he killed a stag, provoking the anger of Artemis because it was the animal sacred to her. In order to have her revenge on him she demanded the sacrifice of Iphigéneia, the king's daughter. Even to the nymph Kallisto, who was numbered amongst her companions and had promised that she would always remain a virgin, her behaviour was no better. The goddess changed her into a bear when she learned that she had become pregnant by Zeus; Kallisto bore Arkas, progenitor of the inhabitants of Arkadia. In the case of Ariadne, daughter of Minos, it is said that Artemis killed her when she submitted to the amorous invitation of Theseus. Furthermore Niobe, who was the daughter of Tantalos and his wife Amphione from Thebes, made the mistake of boasting that she had twelve children - six sons and six daughters – while Leto had only two. Artemis and Apollo took revenge on her by killing all her children; Artemis dealt with the girls, and Apollo the boys.

The Aloades, **Otos** and **Ephialtes**, were giants, the sons of Iphimedeia and Aloas or Poseidon. According to a prophecy, they could not be destroyed, either by the hand of a mortal or a god. Thus once, when they were chasing Artemis in order to lay with her, Apollo sent a stag between them and in their attempts to shoot it they killed each other instead.

Hermes

Thief from his birth

Zeus lay in secret with Maia in a cave at Kyllene and subsequently Hermes was born. Clever, quick, crafty but mainly a cheat and stealer of cattle, he was given to jokes and playing tricks from the very moment of his birth. Still a new-born baby only a few hours old, he got out of his cradle. He had hardly left the cave when he met a tortoise and was fascinated by it. Without losing any time he killed it, took its shell, stretched seven strings made from the gut of animals over it and thus fashioned the first lyre. While he was trying it out and enjoying himself, he became hungry and decided to steal the cattle belonging to his brother, Apollo. He reached Pieria with ease and quickly took fifty cows from the herd, turned them upside down so that a trail of hoofprints would not betray him, and led them near to the Alpheos. There, as they say, fire was first lit in the history of humanity by rubbing a laurel twig against another piece of wood. Having skinned two cows, he butchered them, spitted them and placed them in the fire. When the meat was ready he divided it into twelve portions, one for each god, and despite his hunger and tiredness, left the meat to commemorate his first theft. As soon as it started to get light, the little Hermes extinguished the fire, scattered the ashes, returned to the cave and lay down again in his cradle as if nothing had happened. He told

Around 520 B.C. Hipparchos, the son of Peisistratos, placed stone columns with male members and the head of a bearded man in the streets and at the crossroads in Attica, as place and distance markers. These were called 'Herms' after Hermes, in honour of him as an 'Odio', or way- guide.

his mother, who had knowledge of all that had taken place, that he claimed the same position on Olympos as Apollo and that if Zeus did not give him what he wanted he would become the king of thieves. Meanwhile Apollo, seeing that nothing remained of his herd, quickly realized that his little brother was responsible and set off to find him. Arriving at the cave in Kyllene he found the little one playing nonchalantly in his cradle and when he told him about his cattle he denied, very convincingly, any involvement in the affair. Then Apollo became angry and brought Hermes to Olympos; in front of Zeus, he listed all the tricks and lies of the youngster. The father of the gods burst out laughing, counselled the brothers to make it up and ordered Hermes to take Apollo to his cattle. And so it happened. On the way, Hermes tried to mollify his big brother by playing on his lyre. Apollo listened to the instrument in wonder and was moved. Hermes, who wanted to seem good-hearted, gave his brother the lyre and the latter, to reciprocate, gave him a golden wand (the caduceus), the prophetic ability which the three virgins of Parnassos enjoyed, the power which he had over animals, and his office as conveyor of souls - that is to say, messenger to Hades.

Messenger of Zeus

The god with the wings on his shoulders, feet and cap can justifiably be characterized as a god of the air. Holding the caduceus, the wand with the snakes, he impetuously and quick as the wind relayed the messages and with all speed carried out the wishes of Zeus. Sometimes however, in order to be completely effective, he could become invisible, as in the War of the Giants, wearing the cap known as the 'Aidos kyní'.

*Until the 5th century B.C. Hermes was depicted as a bearded god. He appeared as a young, athletic god for the first time in the Parthenon frieze, and much later in the famous statue at Olympia by the sculptor Praxiteles,, who portrayed Hermes carrying the newly-born Dionysos to the nymphs for them to raise him. The **Hermes of Praxiteles**, c. 330 B.C. Archaeological Museum of Olympia.*

41

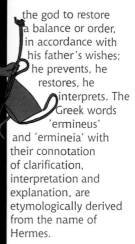

the god to restore a balance or order, in accordance with his father's wishes; he prevents, he restores, he interprets. The Greek words 'ermineus' and 'ermineia' with their connotation of clarification, interpretation and explanation, are etymologically derived from the name of Hermes.

Hermes was a member of the Dionysiac company which undertook to bring Hephaestos back to Olympos.

The lord of the air and spaces carried out the commands of his father by organizing some situations, sorting out others that had become difficult, and accomplishing dangerous missions. He undertook to go down to the underworld and persuade Hades to allow Persephone to return to her mother. When Alcmene the mother of Herakles died, he stole her away and carried her to the Islands of the Blest, where she became the wife of Rhadamanthus. Furthermore Herakles, thanks to Hermes, managed to suckle the milk of Hera, when the latter put him to her breast without

her realizing it. When Zeus fell in love with Ganymede and kidnapped him, he sent Hermes to comfort the boy's father and assure him that his son would become immortal. Hermes saved Io, when Hera had changed her into a cow and assigned the monster Argos Panoptes (the all-seeing) to guard her, as punishment for having become her husband's mistress. He killed the monster whose body was covered with eyes with a single rock, after having lulled all his eyes to sleep; after this he was called Argeïphontes. Thus there are dozens of stories which attest to the intervention of

*A common theme on Attic lekythoi is Hermes leading souls into the underworld. In his identity as **conveyor of souls** and of the dead he brings back Persephone from the Underworld, and steals the dead Alcmene, leading her to the Isles of the Blest.*

Aphrodite

Rising out of the foam

According to Hesiod Uranos, whose wife was Gaia, did not allow his children to live for fear that they would take away his power. When therefore he lay one evening in the arms of his wife, his son Kronos who had made an arrangement with her, cut off his genitals with a scythe and threw them into the sea. They floated and were washed away; thereafter foam was created around them and from that foam there emerged a girl. She was called Aphrodite, meaning 'born from the foam'; she swam off and reached Kythera first and then Cyprus. This most beautiful goddess first came out of the water onto the beach of Paphos and was thus called 'Kypris' (the Cyprian) and 'Kyprogeneia' (born on Cyprus). However, as she had also swum in the waters around Kythera she was in addition known as 'Kythereia', meaning 'the Kytheran'. Another story relates that Aphrodite was not born out of sea foam, but was the daughter of Zeus and Dione.

Irresistible Aphrodite

The lawful wife of Hephaestos did not lose any opportunity for amorous adventures. The most well-known and titillating story is that of her union with Ares and the way in which Hephaestos himself exposed them while they were in bed. With Ares, Aphrodite had four children: Harmony, Deimos, Phobos and Eros. Apart from her own perfidies, however, she took care never to leave others in peace but aroused in them lust for amorous relationships. She was desired by all and her only enemies were Athena, Artemis and Hestia, the two latter goddesses because of their eternal virginity and Hestia because she was the protectoress of marriage. Above all she liked to arouse Zeus' lust for mortal women. In order to stop her from doing this, Zeus

Sandro Botticelli, 1485, Uffizi Gallery, Florence.

Aphrodite
and Ares.

not hold back her passion, conspired with her nurse and went to her father's bed every evening. When the latter realized what had happened, he went to kill her. She ran away to escape and implored the gods to save her; thus they transformed her into a bush, the well-known myrtle. Several months later, a beautiful child issued forth from the myrtle – this was Adonis. Aphrodite took the child and brought it to Persephone for her to bring it up. Persephone fell in love with Adonis, and so

caused her to fall in love with the mortal Anchises. Apart from Zeus, Aphrodite threw many into the web of love in order to wreak her revenge on them. Thus she condemned Eos, who had dared to lay with Ares, to be on aconstant search for new lovers. She did the same with the daughters of Kinyras on Cyprus, making them give themselves to strangers who came to the island.

While Anchises was pasturing his sheep on Ida in the Troad, Aphrodite saw him from afar and was captivated by his beauty. She went, therefore, to Cyprus, dressed and perfumed herself, took the form of a mortal and appeared in front of him. Even though

Anchises immediately realized that she was a god, she assured him that she was mortal and the daughter of Otreus, king of Phrygia. She said that she had been sent by Hermes to be his wife. Thus the passions of Anchises were aroused and he immediately lay with her. Anchises then slept on sweetly, until Aphrodite assumed her true form and awakened him. She told him the truth and that the child that would be born of their union was to be called Aeneas, who would rule in Troy.

She made Myrra or Smyrna, daughter of king Theias, fall in love with her own father because she had neglected to worship her like all the other goddesses. The daughter, who could

*When Adonis was mortally wounded by the wild boar, Aphrodite wept copiously. Roses sprouted from her tears, and from the blood of Adonis there sprang up the plant which bears his name (**Adonis anua**).*

did Aphrodite. In order to prevent them from fighting Zeus decided that he could spend one third of the year with one goddess, one third with the other, and for the last third he could do what he liked. Not much time had passed, however, before Adonis, who was out hunting and attacked by a wild boar, was killed. A tearful Aphrodite begged

The only one not invited to the wedding of Thetis with the mortal Peleas was Eris. In order to make her displeasure known, this goddess, who was the embodiment of discord, threw an apple into the midst of the wedding feast, 'to be given to the most beautiful'. The three great goddesses Hera, Athena and Aphrodite claimed the apple and Zeus was forced to appoint a mortal as a referee; this was Paris. Aphrodite won the apple of beauty because she promised Paris that she would give him Helen, the most beautiful woman in the world.. That is how the Trojan War started, during which Aphrodite was on the side of Paris and all the Trojans. The Judgment of Paris. Marcantonio Raimondi, c. 1516.

Persephone to allow him to come to the upper world for half of the year. She did so, and as a result of this myth Adonis was worshipped as the god of vegetation, regeneration, and spring.

Aphrodite had one son with Poseidon, who was called Erykas and became king of Sicily. She also had one daughter, Rhodos, who gave her name to the island. Aphrodite also fell in love with Dionysos and bore him Priapos, the ugly god of fertility. It was not impossible, some said, that Priapos was the son of Adonis, fathered by him when Dionysos was away on a distant campaign.

The Aphrodite of Melos, c. end of the 2nd century B.C. Louvre, Paris.

The myrtle (**Myrtus communis**) is connected with Aphrodite. When the goddess emerged from the sea at Paphos on Cyprus, she hid behind a myrtle bush to cover her nakedness. Thus the bush became a symbol of youth and beauty.

45

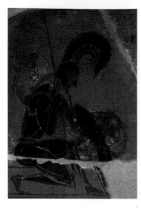

Ares

Warlike tempest

Ares was the only legitimate son of Zeus and Hera. His name is most probably to be identified with the noun áres, which meant 'the weapon of war', or even battle itself. He was born and lived in Thrace, which for the Greeks was a barbarous country. Even though his objective was to a large decree the same as that of his sister Athena, there was a huge difference between the two; Athena embodied wisdom and correct war strategy, while Ares embodied the tempest and the madness of war. Thus the contest that developed between them took on considerable dimensions in the Trojan War, when Ares fought on the side of the Trojans. There, Athena wounded him seriously on two occasions, once at the hand of Diomedes and once by her own hand. When however the god went to complain to Zeus, he did not find any sympathy. The behaviour of the Aloades, Otos and Ephialtes, was shameful towards Ares; they captured him and shut him up in a bronze cauldron for thirteen months. He would have died there from his torment if Hermes had not rescued him.

Ares had one daughter, Alcippe, with Aglauros. When however Alirrothios, the son of Poseidon lusted after her and raped her, Ares killed him. Ares was judged and found not guilty for his deed. The trial took place on a rock to the west of the Acropolis, which from that time on was named the 'Areopagos'.

According to Homer Aphrodite, who was married to Hephaestos, deceived her husband with the god of war. This relationship, which embodies the union of the wild with the temperate, produced Harmony, who was as beautiful as her mother and was taken as a wife by Kadmos, king of Thebes. It is said that other children of this illicit union were Eros and the terrible pair Deimos and Phobos, who accompanied their father in wars. It was their bad luck, however, that the relationship did not remain secret and Hephaestos humiliated them by catching them in the act, binding them with chains which he had forged himself.
Ares and Aphrodite. Sandro Botticelli, 1483. London, National Gallery.

Herakles was not at all afraid to take on Ares. The son of the god, **Kyknos**, was just as bloodthirsty as his father and it was said that he wanted to build a temple from human skulls. When Herakles met him and he tried to take his head, the hero was able to kill him, with the help of Athena. Zeus personally intervened in the battle that ensued between the half-brothers Herakles and Ares - the latter desiring revenge for the loss of his son - and separated the two opponents.

Hephaestos

The unwanted baby

Two legitimate sons were born to Zeus and Hera, and he disliked both of them - Ares because he loved blood and Hephaestos because he was ugly. Let us, however, begin from the beginning, as they say. Hera became pregnant before she actually married Zeus. When she gave birth, either because she wanted to hide the child or because he was very ugly and lame, she threw him into the sea to get rid of him. By his good luck, after tumbling down into the deep for nine days, he fell into the

Dionysos brings Hephaestos back to Olympos.

hands of the Nereid Thetis and the Okeanida Eurynome, who undertook to raise him secretly in the cave of Nereus in the depths of the sea. There, until his ninth year, the god practiced his metallurgical skills, making jewellery for women. Others say that it was not Hera who hurled the child into the sea but Zeus, when the child wanted to take the side of his mother in an argument she had with her husband. He threw him onto Lemnos and the Sidies, a people who lived there, took care of him. The Kabeiri, gods of iron-working, are considered to be the sons or descendants of the Lemnian Hephaestos. As things would have it, the unwanted baby grew up far from his parents and apart from being lame he became fat, tall, and even more ugly.

Retaliation against Hera

When Hephaestos reached the age of nine he wanted to claim the position which belonged to him on Olympos. Having become a very accomplished iron-worker he constructed a golden throne and sent it to his mother as a gift. She was delighted that her son harboured no ill-will; however, when she sat down on it, invisible chains bound her and she could not get up. When all realized that Hephaestos had done this in order to get his revenge, they decided that he would need some coaxing and sent his brother Ares to him, but the fires of Hephaestos did not allow him to approach. The next attempt, which was successful, was made by Dionysos. He plied him with wine, got him drunk and led him on his horse to Olympus. There the gods welcomed him, but the time to release Hera had barely arrived when

Apart from on Lemnos, where Hephaestos was worshipped until the 6th century B.C. in the city of the same name (Hephaistiada), he was also worshipped in Athens. He was venerated there along with Athena, as patron of iron-workers. Later, in 450 B.C. the Athenians built a splendid temple, the Hephaisteion, in the market place of Athens in honour of the two deities; this is widely known as the **Theseion**.

he, although drunk, demanded Aphrodite as his bride in exchange.

It is believed that **Erichthonios**, the first king of Athens, was born from the seed of Hephaestos. It was said that Hephaestos desired Athena and pursued her in order to lay with her. While she was running away from him, his seed fell on her. She brushed it off and it fell onto the soil of Attica; Erichthonios 'sprang up' from it.

Cuckolded husband

Hephaestos might have taken the most desirable of all the goddesses as his wife, but he did not foresee that she, as the goddess of love, would not possibly be satisfied with just being his lawful wife. Among the multitude of her lovers was his own brother Ares, with whom she not only had a relationship but also produced four children – Harmony, Eros, Deimos and Phobos. The first amorous encounter of these deities was said to have been in Hephaestos' own bed and was seen only by the sun, which hastened to the cuckolded husband to bear witness. He was greatly hurt and wanted to

take revenge, so he constructed a web of invisible chains, hung it above the bed and then went off on a journey to Lemnos. After he departed, Ares went to the palace of Hephaestos, found Aphrodite and they prepared to lie together in the bed. So the illicit lovers fell into the trap and as they were bound fast together Hephaestos

The first woman, **Pandora**, was created by Hephaestos. He formed her from earth and water and made her beautiful, hardy, and gave her a voice, according to instructions from Zeus.

49

entered, having brought with him the other gods in order to ridicule Ares and Aphrodite as much as he could. The only one who did not laugh was Poseidon. On the contrary, he demanded that Hephaestos free the two deities and persuaded them to leave. Thus Aphrodite went to Cyprus and Ares to Thrace, to be near to his warlike countrymen.

Hephaestos hands the weapons of Achilles to Thetis.

Wonderful smith

Hephaestos, who had learned to work in metal while he was still in the cave of Nereus, deep in the sea, developed into an excellent craftsman whose hands produced marvellous works. He created the palaces of the gods on Olympos, the bed of the sun, the arrows of Artemis and Apollo, the sceptre of Agamemnon, and the bronze giant Talos. He also fashioned and embellished the arms of the two greatest heroes, Herakles and Achilles. Their shields, made from the most precious of materials, depicted scores of scenes and were so imposing that they were praised as wondrous works.

*When Typhon, edged on by Hera, threatened the power of Zeus, all of the gods changed into animals and left Olympos. Hephaestos did likewise and became a bull. Later on however, when Zeus had defeated Typhon and crushed him beneath Etna on Sicily, Hephaestos established his **workshop** there. Its location in that particular place attests to the connection of the god not only with fire but also with volcanoes, as is shown by his name*

Dionysos

'Twice-born'

Zeus was in love with Semele, one of the daughters of king Kadmos of Thebes. In order to lie with her he entered the palace secretly one evening and stretched out on her bed. Hera, despite the discretion of her husband, noticed everything that happened concerning his new mistress. Knowing that Zeus had promised the king's daughter that he would grant her whatever she desired, Hera, in order to have her revenge, instilled in her the desire to see him in all his majesty. Zeus was unsuccessful in his attempts to dissuade her, so when he appeared before her with an overwhelming brilliance and with his thunderbolt, the palace of Kadmos caught fire and Semele herself was burnt to death. Since she was already six months' pregnant, Zeus took the child to prevent it from being burned and hid it in his thigh until the time came for it to be born. In order to protect the child, Gaia herself made ivy grow from out of the flames. When Dionysos came into the world, so that Hera would not hear about the birth Zeus gave him to Ino, sister of Semele. However, nothing escaped the notice of Hera and in order to have her revenge, she sent Ino and her husband Athamas madness and drove them to burn to death their own children, Learchos and Melikertes.

Zeus managed to save the baby Dionysos by changing him into a goat and sending him with Hermes to the nymphs of Mount Nysa, which might have been somewhere in Asia. It is possible that he gained his name thus: Zeus (Dias) + Nysa = Dionysos. According to another story Dionysos was not the son of Semele but of Demeter or Persephone by Zeus. When the baby was born the Titans, either because they had perceived that he had some connection with the power of Zeus or because Hera put them up

The birth of Dionysos from the thigh of Zeus.

to it, butchered him and ate him. To exact his revenge Zeus burned the Titans to death, while Demeter managed to reconstruct Dionysos from the little pieces of the butchered god.

Viticulturalist and wine-maker

Hera did not relent while Dionysos was growing up in the forests under the care of the nymphs. The abhorrence and hatred which she felt for him led her to drive him mad. Thus began the wanderings of the god in Egypt, Syria and Phrygia. In spite of the fact that he was nursed in Phrygia by Rhea, he did not cease from his travels which were intended to spread the cultivation of the vine. Later on they said that the god even reached far-off India. On his travels he was accompanied by nymphs, satyrs, silenes, and maenads. In Attica, Dionysos taught viticulture and the production of wine to Ikarios, from the area of the same name which is called 'Dionysos' today. However, when Ikarios offered wine to the shepherds of the locality, they became drunk and thought that he was trying to poison them. For this

reason they killed him, and buried him without anyone knowing about it. When his daughter Irigone with the help of her hound, Maira, found the body of her father in a well, she hanged herself in her grief. It is said, too, in Aetolia that Dionysos taught king Oineas to make wine, having taken a fancy to his wife, Althaia, by whom he also had a daughter, Diaeneira.

Bacchus, Michelangelo Buonarroti, 1497.

'Pure' Ariadne

Ariadne, daughter of Minos and Pasiphäe, whose name means both 'sacred' and 'pure', was said to have been the official companion of Dionysos. According to the myth, Ariadne and her ball of thread helped Theseus to kill the Minotaur. Following the demise of the monster, the hero took her with him but abandoned her on the island of Dia (Naxos?), because according to one version of the myth Dionysos appeared to him in a dream and told him that the girl was his. Others said that while Ariadne, abandoned by Theseus, was sleeping, Dionysos appeared and took her for his own. There is also one account which relates that Artemis killed her on Dia. On Naxos they believed that Ariadne gave Dionysos two sons, Staphylos and Oinopion.
Mosaic. Chania, 3rd c. A.D

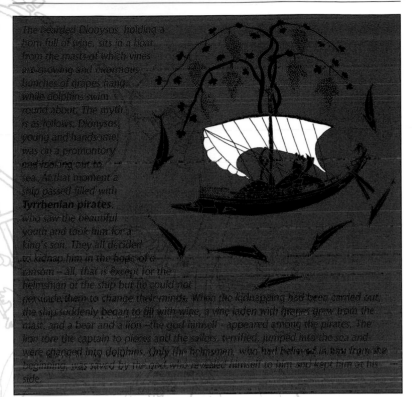

The bearded Dionysos, holding a horn full of wine, sits in a boat from the masts of which vines are growing and enormous bunches of grapes hang, while dolphins swim round about. The myth is as follows. Dionysos, young and handsome, was on a promontory and looking out to sea. At that moment a ship passed filled with **Tyrrhenian pirates**, who saw the beautiful youth and took him for a king's son. They all decided to kidnap him in the hope of a ransom – all, that is except for the helmsman of the ship but he could not persuade them to change their minds. When the kidnapping had been carried out, the ship suddenly began to fill with wine, a vine laden with grapes grew from the mast, and a bear and a lion – the god himself – appeared among the pirates. The lion tore the captain to pieces and the sailors, terrified, jumped into the sea and were changed into dolphins. Only the helmsman, who had believed in him from the beginning, was saved by the god who revealed himself to him and kept him at his side.

Wild feasts

Homer does not seem to attach great importance to Dionysos, since he does not even assign him a place in Olympos; nevertheless, it is certain that his worship began in prehistoric times, since his name has been read on Linear B tablets from Pylos. Wine, dancing and ecstasy are the main components of dionysiac worship which from very early times found resonance among simple people. The festivals held in honour of Dionysos Lysios, the god who helped them forget everyday worries, were many and important: The Lénaia and the Anthestéria were connected with the drinking of wine, the Agriónia was connected with the 'mania' of women, the Agrotiká Dionysia was connected with

The Dionysiac company

In addition to the dionysiac festivals there was a Dionysiac company, its main emblems being branches of ivy and vines and the thyrsos – that is to say a wand which had an ivy leaf and a pine cone on its upper part. The company, faithful to the legend, consisted mainly of the maenads, the satyrs, the silenes, Priapus and Pan. In the mythical retinue there were always wild animals, such as lions, panthers and leopards which had been made docile by the wine.

The **maenads** often wore the skins of stags around their shoulders and performed ecstatic dances. The satyrs and silenes with erect phallus, half-animal and half-man, had horse-like hooves and tails, faces with long beards, flattened noses, and animal ears. Priapos, perhaps the son of Dionysos by some nymph, always obscene and with erect phallus, symbolizes the reproductive power of nature. This god is often depicted as a simple mask, which sometimes has a 'maddened' and sometimes 'mellow' expression.

sacrifices of billy-goats, and the Katagógia with the return of Dionysos from the sea. There was also, of course, the Megála (Great) Dionysia. Based on and within the framework of these festivals the Dithyramb and Tragedy were later developed, and we can say with certainty that the theatre was born out of the worship of Dionysos. Apart from the official festivals, smaller groups carried out religious rites every two years on Parnassos which were called 'orgies'; only women took part in them. These were the maenads who, brandishing a thyrsos (wand) and torches would enter a state of 'hysteria' and run through the fields. From their frenzied madness to unite with Dionysos, they would tear any animal they came across to shreds, in the belief that it was the god in one of his transformations. According to myth, Dionysos punished whoever showed disbelief in the religious rites held in his honour. Thus the god drove mad the three daughters of Minyas, king of Orchomenos, who mocked the female participants in these frenzied celebrations, so that they hacked to pieces one of their children and thereafter rampaged in the mountains until he turned them into birds. Similarly, he sent madness to the daughters of Proitos, king of Tiryns, because they spurned his rites.

LESSER GODS
AND GROUPS OF
DEITIES

Hades
Asklepios
Sky deities
Earth deities
Sea spirits or
Gerontes
Eros

Hades

Hades or Haïdes, invisible god and lord of the shadows

Hades and Persephone.

Hades was one of the three sons of Kronos, along with Zeus and Poseidon; after the drawing of lots he won the control of the Underworld. To that place, which was also called Hades and guarded by a dog, Cerberus, Charon brought the dead in his boat on the river and lake of Acheron. Since the people of antiquity associated the Underworld with the wealth-producing ('plutoparagogikí') power of the Earth, Hades was called Pluton and considered the god of vegetation, productivity and wealth. His wife was Persephone, daughter of Demeter, whom he had kidnapped. Subsequently he agreed with her mother to let her spend eight months above the earth.

Asklepios

The physician who... raised the dead

At some stage, Apollo fell in love with Koronis, daughter of Phlegyas who was the son of Ares and ruled in Lakereia in Thessaly. When he lay with her she had already arranged her marriage with

Statue of Asklepios from the Sanctuary at Epidaurus, 4th century B.C.

Ischys, son of the king of Arkadia. When the time came for the wedding, a white crow took the news to Apollo. The god was so furious that he changed the white bird into a black one, killed Ischys and set Artemis to kill Koronis. Since however she was pregnant, he took the baby just before she died and placed it in the care of the Centaur Cheiron on Pelion, for him to raise it. This baby was Asklepios who

*Head of a statue of **Hygeia**, c. 360 B.C. National Archaeological Museum of Athens.*

was taught how to care for the sick by the wise centaur. However, because he made great progress and began even to raise the dead, he provoked the anger of Zeus who killed him with his own hands, by means of a thunderbolt. The daughters of Asklepios were Ipione, Hygeia, Iaso, Akeso and Panakeia (Panacea); his sons Machaon and Podaleirios are also connected with medicine.

Sky deities

Helios, Selene, Eos, Iris

Helios in his chariot with the winged horses.

Light, darkness, sunrise and sunset, weather phenomena and the seasons generated questions in the minds of men and aroused their fantasies. Thus they fashioned deities which were rulers of space and responsible for these phenomena. In the orb of the sun with its golden rays they saw the face and golden hair of a god whom they named **Helios**. Since he crosses the vault of the sky every day they believed that he sat in a chariot of fire drawn by two or four horses and travelled daily from his palace in the east to his palace in the west. At night, a winged bed or a golden cup carried him from west to east. According to Hesiod, Helios, Selene and Eos were grandchildren of Uranos and Gaia and children of the Titans Hyperion and Theia. With the Okeanida Perse, Helios produced Circe and Aeëtes, father of Medea, and with Klymene, wife of Merops, king of Ethiopia, he produced Phaethon. When the latter grew up, in order to persuade Helios to acknowledge him as a son, he asked to be able to drive the golden chariot. Helios gave it to him but the horses bolted and Zeus killed the young charioteer. Helios was also passionately in love with Rhodos, with whom he produced three sons, and with Neiara on whom he fathered daughters, the Heliades, who tended his sacred herds. His role in the War of the Giants and in the Trojan War was ancillary; he carried out the orders of Zeus and Hera, first of all bringing the dawn later -as instructed by Zeus - and then bringing sunset later, following Hera's desire that the war should cease.

Selene, whose name means 'brilliant', was the sister of Helios; according to some she was his wife. They believed that she bore him the Hours - the seasons of the year. There is yet another story

Selene travels during the night in her winged chariot.

The third sister, **Eos**, goddess of the dawn, is also represented in a winged chariot. She fell in love with the handsome Tithonos and asked Zeus to make him immortal. However, when he grew old, she did not want him any more. He became ugly and wrinkled, but did not die and only his voice could be heard. Therefore, Eos changed him into a cicada. With him she produced Memnon, later king of Ethiopia, and Imathion. Eos also loved the giant Orion, Kleito, and Kephalos, son of Hermes and Erse.

*The messenger of the gods gave her name to the Iris plant (**Iris unguicularis**).*

that Selene had an amorous relationship with Endymion which produced fifty daughters, and also one with goat-hoofed Pan. Like Helios, **Selene** was originally represented in a winged chariot. Later on she was depicted on horseback, or riding a mule, bull, stag or goat.

The winged **Iris**, granddaughter of Pontos and Okeanos and daughter of Thaumas and Elektra, was the messenger of the gods. She personified the rainbow which connected the sky and the earth, and was thus originally considered to be a connective link and messenger between mortals and immortals. She is depicted wearing a short tunic, winged sandals and holds a caduceus in her hand.

Earth deities

Gaia, Rhea, Cybele, Pan, Priapos

In the beginning, according to Hesiod, there was the Earth, Chaos, and Eros. The Earth gave birth to Pontos (the sea), the mountains and Uranos (the sky) with whom she united and brought forth the Titans, the Cyclops and the Ekatoncheires (the Hundred-Handed Ones). She formed an alliance with one of her sons, the Titan Kronos, and managed to put aside Uranos who kept his children imprisoned so that they would not usurp him. Thus Kronos seized power from him, but was fated to live with the same threat: one of his children would take his throne. Whenever his wife Rhea gave birth he gobbled up the child until she herself, like Gaia, devised a plan to save her last child, Zeus, and help him to become king of the gods. Rhea was a Titan, daughter and daughter-in-law of Gaia; she gave Kronos, who was her brother and husband, a stone, pretending that it was their new-born child. As mother and Great Goddess, Rhea exhibits many similarities with Gaia and with her daughters, Demeter and Hera.

Cybele, a foreign import from Phrygia to Greece, exhibits the characteristics of motherhood and of fertility. Goddess of fruitfulness and verdant growth, but also of the mountains and of wild animals, she was worshipped in the countryside with ecstatic dances and depicted with her favourite animal, the lion. Together with Cybele and Dionysos, goat-footed Pan, the hideously ugly god with horns and pointed ears, roamed the mountains dancing and singing. He was the son of Hermes and a nymph, who promptly abandoned him after his birth on account of his ugliness. The god who invented the 'panpipes' – the flute made from reeds – has a mad reproductive urge and managed to lay with Selene herself, covered with a fleece. The deity associated with fecundity par excellence was Priapos, the god with the enormous phallus. Ugly, old, and often exhibiting zoomorphic characteristics, such as ram's horns, he lived in the countryside and protected animals and plants. According to one account he was the son of Aphrodite by Dionysos or by Zeus.

Representation of Aphrodite and Pan, c. 100 B.C. National Archaeological Museum of Athens.

Rhea

Sea deities, 'Old Men of the Sea'

Nereus, Proteus, Triton, Glaukos

The sea deities, otherwise called sea 'daemons', were illusive spirits with magic and prophetic capabilities and also the ability to transform themselves. One of these, Nereus, was the son of Gaia and Pontos and married Doris who was the daughter of Okeanos and Tethys. He had fifty daughters with her; these were the Nereids who were nymphs of the waters. He was called 'the old man of the sea', either because he was the first child of Pontos, or because he was wise and famous for his love of truth and his justice. Proteus came from the East, founded his own kingdom in Thrace, married and had two sons, Telegonos and Polygonos. When Herakles came to Thrace and killed his sons, Proteus threw himself into the sea from grief. From then on he became a water-sprite and sailors, to show him respect, called him 'old man of the sea'. There are many myths concerning his prophetic capabilities and in particular his ability to change himself into an animal or whatever element of nature he wished.

Triton was a sea spirit, son of Poseidon and Amphitrite; his name probably means 'water'. Half-man and half-fish, he lived constantly in the sea, taking care of his father's chariot, dallying with the Nereids and making beautiful sounds by blowing into seashells. Glaukos was a mortal - a fisherman - until one day he discovered by chance a plant that wrought wonders and thus became a god. He is represented as a man with seaweed and shells on his body and was considered to have great prophetic ability. Indeed, some said that he taught Apollo the art of prophecy.

Eros

Hesiod states that the first to be created was Chaos, then Earth, and thereafter **Eros**. According to his view, therefore, Eros was not born of any individual, but he was a primordial power, fundamental to the evolution of the Greek cosmogony. Others believed that Eros was the son of Aphrodite and Ares and that he instigated the amorous coexistence of couples. He was imagined and described as young, naked, with golden wings, and said to shoot his arrows at both the gods and men, arousing their hearts and awakening their erotic appetites.

The Muses

Zeus was in love with his aunt, the Titan Mnemosyne, who was the daughter of Uranos and Gaia. After they lay together for nine whole nights,

Mnemosyne gave birth, in Pieria, to nine daughters who had only music, dance and song in their minds. They were called Muses and were named Kleio, Euterpe, Thaleia, Melpomene, Terpsichore, Erato, Polymnia, Urania and Kalliope. In later times they were associated with writing and the arts and each one was the embodiment of a particular sphere of literature or art.

The Three Graces, Raphael, 1504-5. Musée Condé, Chantilly.

The Graces

With his cousin the Okeanida Eurynome, who was the daughter of Okeanos and Tethys, Zeus produced the Graces ('Hárites'),

three very beautiful daughters who were represented in the nude, two of them looking towards the onlooker and the one in the middle with her back turned. As their collective name indicates, they spread joy and are connected with fertility and verdant growth. Their names were Aglaia, Euphrosyne and Thaleia. They kept company with and dressed Aphrodite, and spent their life on Olympos dancing and singing.

The Three Graces, Antonio Canova, 1813/16, Hermitage Museum.

Apollo and Nymphs, Girardon, c. 1670, Versailles.

The Nymphs

The nymphs were daughters of Zeus, spirits of the woods, the rivers and the streams. In various accounts we hear of beautiful girls who kept company with Artemis in the wilds of the mountains and were venerated in caves and on altars beside springs. They are connected with gods and heroes, either as mothers – for example there was Maia who, with Zeus, produced Hermes, and Kallisto who bore Arkas; or they acted as wet-nurses, as for Zeus, Dionysos and Aeneas. They are closely collected with verdant growth and it was believed that when a nymph was born a tree sprouted at the same time and then withered at the hour of her death. Some nymphs, such as the Dryads and the Amadryads, were both trees and women at the same time. Their association with water as an essential element of growth derives from their connection with trees. This is the reason why they were often believed to be daughters of Okeanos and the rivers. The water nymphs were called 'Naiads' and the nymphs of the mountains 'Oreiads'.

The Nereids

The fifty beautiful daughters of Nereus, son of Pontos and Gaia, with the Okeanida Doris, were called Nereids. They lived exclusively in the depths of the sea, near their father, and amused themselves by dancing and singing with their nephew Triton, son of Amphitrite and Poseidon, and other mythical sea creatures. They constantly intervened in the development of weather phenomena and especially when there were storms, helping sailors, heroes, and even gods. The most well-known of the fifty sisters are Thetis, wife of the mortal Peleus and mother of Achilles, and Amphitrite, wife of Poseidon. We meet them a number of times as wet-nurses or nannies who undertake the upbringing of infants, such as Hephaestos and Dionysos.

The Okeanides

The three thousand Okeanides were the daughters of Okeanos and Tethys and sisters of the three thousand rivers. They greatly resemble the Nymphs and the Nereids and on the basis of the 41 names given to them by Hesiod, we can discern many of their various characteristics. Some are said to be generous and 'nurturing', being concerned therefore with the upbringing of children (Polydore, Doris, Pluto). Others are identified with the watery element and their names include 'rhoë', meaning 'stream' (Kallirrhoë, Aphirrhoë), or with the swift flow of water (Okyrhoë) or the mystery of water (Kalypso). Others personified exactly what their name suggests: Peitho (the persuader), Xanthi (the blonde-haired), Tyche (luck) etc.

The Hours

Zeus lay with the Titan Themis, who was his aunt and whose name means 'the laws of nature', and fathered the Hours. Their collective name signifies maturity and ripeness, the appropriate moment in time, and it was they who, as the seasons of the year, brought the fruits of the earth. They were beautiful, and lived on Olympos alongside Zeus; they danced, sang and robed Aphrodite. Their names were Eunomia, Dike and Irene, and according to Hesiod they protected the works of men. Thus, apart from being goddesses of verdant growth and fertility, as their names indicate they represented social and political order.

The Fates (Moires)

Hesiod informs us that, in addition to the Hours, Zeus also fathered the Fates with the Titan Themis. Their names – Klotho, Lachesi and Atropos - indicate that they embody all that is designated as the fate of man: the

The Hours

first of them 'spins the thread of life', the second 'apportions' and the third 'cuts the thread of life'. Nobody could interrupt their work, and even Zeus was not able to prevent the death of his son Sarpedon, and of Hektor. Apart from the triad mentioned by Hesiod, philological tradition sometimes mentions two Fates and sometimes four, with the addition of Tyche. Still elsewhere, it is recorded that the Fates were not the daughters of Zeus and Themis, but of Night. In this case they embodied destructive and harmful elements while in the other, as daughters of Themis, the law and order of nature.

The Furies

These are wild spirits who avenged wrongs by causing confusion in the brain. Monsters, with snakes coming out of their hair and blood streaming from their eyes, they scream and move as a group, clothed in grey. They were born from the blood that fell on the earth when Kronos cut off the genitals of his father, Uranos. Some said that they were the daughters of Night. The Furies, whose names were Megaira, Alykto and Tisiphone, pursued Orestes who in anger and retribution for the murder of his father killed his own mother, Clytemnestra. When he was pronounced innocent by the Areopagos, they received an assurance from Athena that he would secure theIr worship in Athens; from that time on they were called the Eumenides.

The Sirens

Malicious beings, half-woman and half-bird, the Sirens bewitched all who heard their enchanting songs and made them forget everything. They were the daughters of Phorkys, son of Pontos and Gaia, or according to others, of the river Acheloos and the Muse Terpsichore, and lived on an island called Anthemoessa. Hapless passers-by forgot not only their homeland and family; they also forgot to eat, thus perishing on the island where the malicious Sirens lived. Circe prepared Odysseus for the difficulties he would experience when passing their island. When his ship drew near to its perilous shores, he stopped the ears of his comrades with wax and made them bind him hand and foot to the ship's mast. Thus they escaped just as the Argonauts had done, thanks to the sound of Orpheus' lyre which drowned out the witches' songs.

THE HEROES

Theseus
Herakles
Kadmos
Oedipus
Jason and Medea
Meleager
Bellerophon
Pelops
Perseus

THE HEROES

In addition to the 'Mythology of the Gods', there is the 'Mythology of the Heroes'. The Heroes differ from the gods in that they are presented as historical personages who existed somewhere between the world of the mortals and immortals. Although today 'heroic' means 'brave', in the epics of Homer this description has a plethora of connotations. The brave warriors are of course heroes, but so are kings, the founders of cities and even some craftsmen and poets. The epic hero is always handsome, clever, dashing and strong. He is often of divine descent in that one of his parents was a deity, but for all the protection that the latter afforded, he is independent, with his own will and initiative.

Theseus

His descent

The first rulers of Athens were Kekrops, Kranaos and Erichthonios who sprang up from the seed of Hephaestos when it fell on the ground during the attempts of the god to lay with the goddess Athena. Erichthonios was succeeded by his son Pandion, and he in turn by Erechtheus who had seven children by Praxithea, daughter of Kifissos. One of these, Kekrops, succeeded Erechtheus. There followed Pandion, son of Kekrops, and his grandson Aegeus who some said was the adoptive son of Pandion. Aegeus took power over Athens but after two marriages he realised that he could not produce children; thus he resolved to visit the oracle at Delphi. There, the Pythia told him not to open his wineskin before he reached Athens; he decided to go to Troizen and ask the king there for his opinion on the oracle. Pittheus, however, made him drunk and set him to lie with his daughter Aethra, who had slept with Poseidon the previous night. When it was announced to Aegeus that Aethra was pregnant, he hid his sandals and sword there and asked her to give them to the child, if it were to be a boy, when he grew up, and send him to Athens. That child was named Theseus and he was the son of Aegeus or of Poseidon; when he was sixteen Aethra revealed to him his father's gifts. Theseus put on the sandals, took up the sword, and set off for Athens.

Aegeus at the Delphic oracle.

Aegeus welcomes Theseus to Athens.

and then departed for Eleusis where he defeated the hitherto unconquered wrestler Kerkyon. There then followed the clash with Prokrustes who lived on the Sacred Way, in the locality known today as Daphni. The latter invited passers-by in and offered them hospitality - short people were given a long bed and tall people a short one; he would then hit the former on the head with a hammer and stretch them, and in the case of the latter he would hack off the

The road to power

On the way to Athens, he had barely arrived in Epidauros when he met Perlphetes, the son of Hephaestos and Antikleia, who killed passers-by with his iron club. Theseus killed him and continued on to Kenchryes, home of the robber Sinis, son of Poseidon. Sinis, whom they called 'Pityokamptis' (bender of pines) would bend two pines together, tie a passer-by to the two tips of the trees, and let them spring back taut, stretching and ripping apart his victim. Having

destroyed Sinis by the robber's very own method, he continued into the region called Krommyonas and there confronted the wild boar named Phaia. Further on, he reached the Rocks

Theseus and Procrustes.

of Skiron, home of the terrible Skiron who forced passers-by to wash his feet and then promptly tossed them into the sea with a kick, where they were torn apart by a sea turtle. Theseus paid him back in his own coin

overhanging limbs. Theseus destroyed him using his very own method, and finally arrived In his father's homeland, Athens.

Theseus and Sinis.

Theseus in Athens

It was July when Theseus entered Athens and the family of the hero Phytalos undertook to cleanse him of the slayings he had carried out. Then he went on to the palace of Aegeus where his father lived with Medea and their son Medos. After he had recognized the sword and with it his son, Aegeus exiled Medea to Colchis because of attempts by the sorceress to poison the heir to the throne. The arrival of Theseus incensed not only Medea but also his fifty kinsmen, the sons of Pallas; thinking that Aegeus had no heir, they had hoped to take the throne. They devised a strategy to seize power by force but were defeated by the clever young heir, who also managed to win a declaration of his innocence in the trial that followed for the murder of his kin.

Battle of the Centaurs. Metope from the south side of the Parthenon. British Museum.

Theseus, the Bull of Marathon and Pirithoos

After having won against his adversaries, Theseus resolved to free Athens from a fierce bull that was causing terrible destruction at Marathon. They said that Herakles had brought the bull from Crete. When he went to Marathon he was caught in a rain shower and sought hospitality from an old woman called Ekale. The following day he set out to face the fierce animal. Having succeeded, he took the animal, now tamed, back with him and on his way decided to stop at the house of the old woman, but she had died in the meantime. When he arrived at Athens, he sacrificed the bull to Apollo Delphinios and in memory of Ekale gave her name to a village in Attica. This achievement of Theseus set the stage for the famous friendship between him and Pirithoos, the king of a people in Thessaly who were called Lapiths.

Pirithoos and Theseus attack the Amazon Andromache.

This is what happened: Pirithoos heard of the brave deed of Theseus and in order to test him stole the cattle that were grazing at Marathon. Theseus pursued him and when the two came face to face, instead of fighting they gave each other their hand and swore eternal friendship. At the wedding of Pirithoos with Hippodameia, the Centaurs who had been invited as his half-brothers became drunk and fell on the Lapith women; a terrible struggle began in which Theseus helped the Lapiths win and drive the Centaurs from those parts. The dedication and close friendship of the two heroes was expressed through all the difficulties they encountered. Together, they participated in the voyage of the Argonauts, the battle against the Amazons and the hunt for the Kalydonian Boar.

Theseus, Minos and the Minotaur

Theseus wanted to rid Athens of the tribute that it paid every year to Minos, offering seven youths and seven maidens as food for the terrible monster, the Minotaur. This tribute was in payment for the loss of Androgeos, son of Minos, who had tried unsuccessfully to kill the bull of Marathon. To achieve his goal, Theseus would have to kill the monster in the Labyrinth.

Despite the objections of his mother, he decided to go down to Crete as one of the victims. Aegeus, also unable to dissuade him, gave the captain of the ship an order; if his son was successful, he was to replace the black sails of the ship with white ones on the return journey home. When the ship arrived in Crete Ariadne, daughter of Minos and Pasiphäe, fell in love with Theseus at the instigation of Aphrodite and promised to help him to escape from the Labyrinth, that intricate building constructed by Daedalos, if he would take her as his wife. They made an agreement between them, and Ariadne tied a ball of wool at the entrance and then

gave it to him so that he would be able to find his way out again. Theseus went into the Labyrinth, killed the monster and was able, with the help of the thread, to get out of the labyrinthine building. He immediately collected Ariadne and the other young people and, having opened holes in the boats of the Cretans so that they would not follow them, embarked on his ship and set sail for Athens. On the way back they stopped on Naxos, where Dionysos fell in love with Ariadne and asked Theseus to leave her there so that he could marry her. Thus, either because that was what he himself wanted or it was instilled in him by Athena, Theseus went off, leaving Ariadne asleep on the island. When they drew near to Athens, nobody remembered to change the sails according to the instructions of Aegeus. When the latter saw the black sails he hurled himself into the sea and from then on it was named the Aegean Sea.

Theseus, king of Athens

When Theseus arrived in Athens he pleased the gods by making sacrifices in gratitude for the success he had had on Crete. Unfortunately, the awful nature of the death of his father remained with him. After the period of mourning and lamentation, Theseus succeeded Aegeus and became the new king of Athens. His first concern was to unite the communities of Attica into one state, centred on Athens. Thus, he divided the citizens into three classes: the nobles, those who possessed land, and those engaged in a business, and he minted coins. He ruled democratically and held absolute power only at times of war. Furthermore, he concentrated on benevolence towards his people and hospitality towards strangers.

While Theseus lies with Ariadne, Athena exhorts him to abandon her.

Antiope and Phaedra: the wives of Theseus

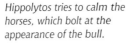

Theseus took part in the campaign of Herakles against the Amazons. One of the latter, Antiope, fell in love with him and helped them win.

Hippolytos tries to calm the horses, which bolt at the appearance of the bull.

Theseus took her to Athens and with her produced Hippolytos; this development provoked the Amazons to attack Attica. In the battle, Antiope was killed fighting at the side of her beloved. Afterwards the king of Athens married Phaedra, the daughter of Minos, and they produced Akamas and Demophon. In the meantime, he sent his first son, Hippolytos, to Troizen to succeed his grandfather. On a visit to Athens, his stepmother Phaedra fell in love with him and sent him a love-letter. When Hippolytos denied her his love she killed herself, fearing that he would betray her to Theseus. She did not hesitate, however, to leave her husband a note in which, twisting the truth, she said that Hippolytos had molested her. Theseus was furious and asked Poseidon for revenge on the youth. While Hippolytos was returning to the Peloponnese in his chariot, a bull suddenly appeared in front of it, causing his horses to bolt. The charioteer was thrown out, and dragged along to his death.

Representation of Theseus and Antiope from the western pediment of the temple of Apollo Daphnoforos at Eretria, c. 510 B.C. Museum of Eretria.

Helen, Hades, and the death of Theseus

After the death of Phaedra, Theseus agreed with Pirithoos that they would marry the daughters of gods. When therefore they set eyes on Helen of Sparta, she was pleasing to them and they kidnapped her. After drawing lots, she fell to Theseus; they then went down to Hades to take Persephone for Pirithoos. There, Pluto made them sit on the chair of Lethe from which it was impossible to rise; they would have stayed there for good if Herakles had not freed them. Returning to Athens, Theseus found that Menestheus, a descendant of Erechtheus, had assumed power. Therefore, he decided to leave and go to Skyros where Lykomedes, whom Theseus considered his friend, hurled him off a cliff and killed him.

Herakles

His descent and birth

Herakles, the son of Alcmene and Amphitryon, or more accurately of Zeus, was born in Thebes. The clan of his mother and of his earthly father actually hailed from the Argolid. To be exact, both were grandchildren of Perseus – Amphitryon as the son of Alkaios, king of Tiryns, and Alcmene as the daughter of Elektryon, king of Mycenae. At some point the Teleboes, sons of Pterelaos and descendants of Perseus, claimed power at Mycenae and killed the eight sons of Elektryon. Then Elektryon handed power to Alcmene and his nephew Amphitryon who, through a mistake, became the cause of the death of Elektryon. His demise gave the other brother, Sthenelos, the opportunity to take power in Mycenae and drive out Amphitryon, who together with Alcmene was exiled to Thebes. Alcmene consented to be the wife of Amphitryon after he promised that he would take revenge on the Teleboes for the loss of her father and brothers.

While Amphitryon was on his way to Ionia, Zeus found an opportunity to lie with Alcmene. It was said that he appeared before her in the guise of her husband. He lay with her, as did Amphitryon himself shortly afterwards when he returned victorious from the battle with the Teleboes. Thus a little while later Alcmene gave birth to twins – Herakles and Iphikles, the former fathered by Zeus and the latter by Amphitryon. On the day that the birth was to take place Zeus had declared that the child who would come into the world first would be king and

The lineage of Herakles

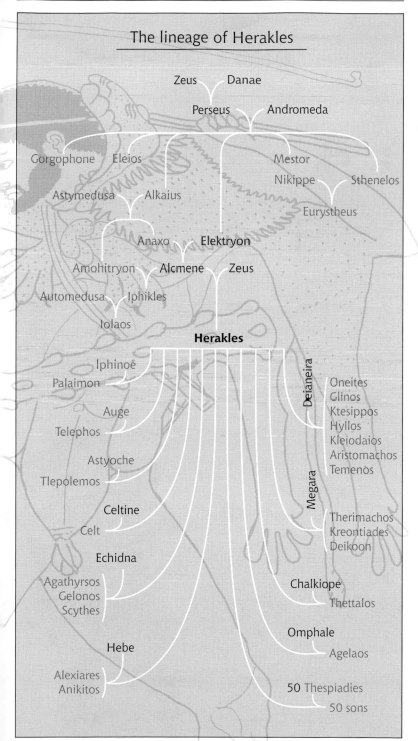

rule over all those who came from his tribe. For this reason, Hera set the goddess of childbirth, Eileithyia, to delay the birth of Herakles and instead to accelerate that of Eurystheus, son of Sthenelos and Nikippe, so that he would be king and Herakles would enter his service until he had fulfilled the twelfth of a series of labours. Even that was not enough; she sent snakes into Herakles cradle to devour him but he succeeded in strangling them, demonstrating his courage even at the very dawn of his life. Despite her wiles, Hera was tricked by Hermes and without realizing it she fed the new-born infant with her own milk; he put the child to her breast while she was sleeping. It was said that as soon as she realized what had happened, she instantly thrust the child away and the Milky Way was formed from the milk that was spilled. According to another account Alcmene, fearing the anger of Hera, tossed the child as soon as he was born into a forest through which Athena and Hera happened to be passing. Athena found and admired the baby and persuaded Hera to feed him. Thus, Herakles was able to drink the milk of the great goddess and secure his immortality.

The childhood and early years of the hero

Herakles grew up in Thebes. Apart from learning to write and play the lyre from Linos, the son of Apollo, he was also taught how to shoot with a bow and arrow, drive a chariot, and wrestle. Some said that he did not learn to write easily and thus his father sent him to mount Kithairon to live amongst the shepherds of his flocks. There, he killed the terrible lion which had devoured the sheep of Amphitryon and of Thespios, king of the Thespians. The latter wondered at his courage and wished to acquire a grandson by him; accordingly he offered him hospitality and sent his fifty daughters to lay with him. All except one, who later became the priestess of his sanctuary, bore children who later colonized Sardinia.

Apart from his wanderings on Kithairon Herakles

roamed over Helikon, the other mountain of Boeotia, where it is said he tore up a wild olive tree and made his famous club from it. When he was eighteen years old, carrying his club in his hand and with the skin of the lion on his shoulders, he returned to Thebes where Creon was king. On the way he met the envoys of Erginos, the king of Orchomenos, who were going to Thebes to collect the annual tax of one hundred head of cattle. This tax was levied as a result of the defeat of Thebes in its conflict with Orchomenos, which had taken place because at some time in the past Menoikeus, the father of Creon, had killed Klymenos, the king of Orchomenos and father of Erginos. When Herakles heard the story he was angry; he cut off the noses and ears of the envoys and sent them to Erginos. When subsequently the Minyans of

*Herakles, with the help of his trusted friend and nephew **Iolaos**, manages to accomplish many of the difficult tasks assigned to him.*

Orchomenos attacked, Herakles defeated them single-handed and after his victory Creon gave him power over Thebes, as well as his daughter Megara for a wife.

At the orders of Eurystheus

While they were living happily in Thebes, Hera suddenly drove him mad and made him kill his own family. When he came to his senses again and saw what he had done he went to the oracle at Delphi from which he received a pronouncement that in order to be cleansed he must go to Mycenae and serve king Eurystheus for twelve years. He was also told that he would perform amazing feats and thus become immortal. Eurystheus, fearing that Herakles would seize power from him, set him a series of very difficult missions, in the hope that on one of them he would perish. Nevertheless, Herakles accomplished the famous twelve labours, which established him as a panhellenic hero.

*When Herakles was on the point of killing his own teacher, **Linos**, his father sent him into the mountains to tend the flocks.*

The Twelve Labours

The Nemean lion

In the locality of Nemea near Mycenae, there lived in a cave a fearsome lion which was

said to have been born by Echidna and her own son, the dog Orthos. Herakles resolved to kill this lion, which was spreading terror over the countryside. Before he arrived at Nemea, he stopped at the city of Kleonai where he was the guest of Molorchos,

a farmer whose son had fallen victim to the lion. Molorchos gave him information as to how he might confront the beast and wanted to sacrifice a boar in his honour. Herakles told him to wait thirty days and then, if he did not return, to sacrifice it. He set off for the cave and some say that he took thirty days to reach its depths where the lion had its lair. After a tough battle with it, he throttled it with his bare hands. Then he skinned it, donned the pelt as a suit of armour, along with a garland of wild celery, and set off on his return. In commemoration of his victory contests were later inaugurated; these were called the Nemean Games

and victors there were crowned with a garland of wild celery.

The Lernaian Hydra

The next monster that Herakles had to face was also an offspring of Echidna, this time with Typhoon. It was called the Lernaian Hydra because it inhabited a place near to the lake of Lerna and was a water-snake with nine heads. Flames emitted from its mouth and poisonous breath from its nostrils. Herakles took Iolaos, his nephew, with him on this difficult mission. When they arrived at Lerna and provoked the appearance of the monster by shooting flaming arrows into its nest, it attacked Herakles. He chopped off its heads with a sickle but this was to no avail, because new heads immediately sprang up. He therefore sent Iolaos to set fire to the forest and bring flaming torches. WIth these he immediately cauterized the wound each time he cut off a head and thus stopped the blood from giving birth to new heads. The last head, which was immortal, he threw on the ground and crushed with a heavy stone. Thus he defeated the monster and by dipping his arrows in its poisonous blood, made them deadly.

The Keryneian Hind

The next mission decreed by Eurystheus was for Herakles to bring back live to Mycenae the hind with the golden horns, which lived on Mount Keryneia on the border between Achaia and Arkadia. The hind caused great damage to the fields, but as its golden horns demonstrated, it was no ordinary animal. Some said that it had been Taygeta, a companion of Artemis whom the latter had changed into a hind because Zeus had desired her; thus she had escaped his clutches. The divine hind was impossible to catch, not only because she ran very swiftly but also because she passed through unknown lands from which nobody had ever returned. Herakles started to chase her from Arkadia, to Adriatica and then to the land of the Hyperboreans, taking care not to injure her. When the hind tried to cross the river Ladon, Herakles closed in and caught her. He tied her feet and took the road home. Then he met Artemis, who was furious because he had captured her sacred animal. Herakles, however, explained that he was merely carrying out the orders of Eurystheus to take the hind to him alive.

The Erymantheian boar

Eurystheus commanded Herakles to bring him live the Erymantheian boar, the terrible wild beast that lived on Mount Erymanthos in Arkadia. Herakes went up the mountain and began to call out as he went in all directions, prompting the boar to keep moving for countless hours over the snows. When the beast was exhausted Herakles caught it with a noose, bound it tightly, hoisted it on his shoulders and brought it to Eurystheus. They say that the latter was so terrified that he hid himself in a pithos that he had sunk into the earth.

The Stymphalian Birds

In the dense forest by the Stymphalian Lake in northern Arkadia there lived some wild birds with long legs and iron wings whose tips were so sharp that they killed their victims with them. These terrible monsters fed on human flesh. As they spread terror by devouring men and plants in the fields, Eurystheus ordered Herakles to destroy them. Athena supported him on this difficult mission giving him a pair of metal rattles, wrought by Hephaestos, which would help him to lure the birds from their hiding-place. So Herakles went up onto a hill and shook the rattles and the birds flew out in fear. Then he began to shoot them with his bow and arrow, one after the other. They say those which escaped took refuge on Mars Island in the Black Sea.

The Stalls of Augeias

Augeias, son of Helios, was king of Elis. At his opulent palace this king of the glittering eyes kept huge herds of cows; their dung had not only filled the stalls but was in danger of polluting the whole area. Therefore, Eurystheus sent Herakles to clean out the dung from the stalls of Augeias, and do it within the space of a day. Herakles presented himself to Augeias and without mentioning Eurystheus, asked for one tenth of the herd if he were to manage to clean out the stalls in a single day. An agreement was made with Phyleas, son of Augeias, as witness. Digging a huge ditch, Herakles diverted two rivers, the Alpheios and the Peneios, through the stalls and achieved the impossible. When however he sought his reward from the king, the latter refused with the excuse that he had been forced into the agreement. Eurystheus also refused to acknowledge the labour had been accomplished when he heard of the way in which Herakles had cleaned the stalls. Later, the hero took his revenge on Augeias by organizing a campaign against Elis in which the king was killed.

The Cretan Bull

As we know, Zeus kidnapped Europa disguised as a bull and brought her on his back from Phoenicia to Crete. Some said that he did not transform himself but that the two came to Crete with the help of a bull. When they arrived they set the bull free but later the gods drove it mad and it began to cause destruction on the island. Eurystheus set Herakles to catch the bull and bring it to him alive. Thus Herakles left for Crete where he informed Minos of the reason for his visit. He began to pursue the bull and at some moment was able to take it by the horns and bind its snout and one of its legs with a rope. He hoisted it onto his shoulders and after saying farewell to Minos, went to Eurystheus. The king was captivated by the beauty of the bull and wanted to dedicate it to Hera. She however, in order not to contribute to the fame of Herakles whom she hated, released the animal, which started to wreak havoc until it arrived at Marathon. Amongst its victims was Androgeos, son of Minos. Theseus saved Athens from the terrible beast.

The Horses of Diomedes

Diomedes, son of Ares, ruled in Thrace which was the home of the warlike people called Bistones. He kept four horses tethered by thick chains in his stables; they fed on human flesh and fire blazed out from their nostrils. Eurystheus ordered Herakles to bring them to him alive. Herakles took other heroes with him on this difficult mission; among them was his friend Abderos. When they arrived in Thrace Herakles went immediately to the stables, killed the guards, stole the horses and took them back to his ship for Abderos to guard. A fight subsequently ensued with Diomedes and his soldiers, who had by then discovered the theft. Herakles killed Diomedes in the battle, but when he returned to his ship he found that Abderos had been devoured by the horses. To honour the friend who had met such a terrible end, Herakles founded a city and named it after him.

The cattle of Geryon

A new order issued by Eurystheus was for Herakles to bring him the red-haired cattle of Geryon, a monster with three bodies which Kallirhoe had born to Crysaor. The cattle were to be found on an island called Erytheia and were guarded by Eurytion and his monstrous dog Orthos. Herakles, after many adventures, crossed Europe and arrived at the strait which separates it from Africa. After having raised the 'pillars of Hercules' there, in order to cross the sea, he made use of the golden cup of Helios

The belt of Hippolyta

Hippolyta was queen of the warlike Amazons who lived in the city of Themiskyra, near the Black Sea. As a symbol of her power she had a belt, which had been a gift from her father. Eurystheus wanted it and ordered Herakles to bring it to him. The latter gathered together some brave comrades and set off on the long journey. On the way, they stopped on Paros where four sons of Minos were living. As the latter murdered two of his comrades, Herakles killed them as well and laid siege to the island. With two prisoners of war he resumed his journey to the land of the Amazons. Hippolyta welcomed him there and promised to give him the belt. However, Hera had changed

herself into an Amazon and let it be known that Herakles had come to seize power, thus the Amazons took up their weapons and launched a frenzied attack on Herakles and his comrades. In the melée which ensued, he killed Hippolyta and snatched her belt. Having decimated the army of the Amazons, he set off for Mycenae and after several adventures, handed over to Eurystheus the belt which he had so coveted.

Herakles travelled to Erytheia in the golden "cup" of the sun.

to sail to Erytheia, where he immediately killed Orthos and the shepherd with his club and stole the cattle. Geryon heard the news and ran to stop him, but he killed him with his arrow. Then Herakles took the road home. He gave back the cup to Helios and having faced many difficulties on the way, including the thief Kakos in Sicily, Scylla, and the snake-woman in Scythia, he arrived at Mycenae and presented the cattle to Eurystheus.

Cerberos

The guardian of Hades, Cerberos was the offspring of Echidna and Typhoon; he was a monster with three dog's heads and a tail which had the head of a snake at its tip. Eurystheus ordered Herakles to bring the animal to him. He was accompanied by Athena and Hermes on this difficult journey to the world of the dead. After he had met a number of the dead and released Theseus, he asked Pluto and Persephone to 'lend' him Cerberos for one day, in order to take him to the Upper World. They agreed on condition that only his hands but no weapons would touch the dog. Herakles indeed managed to tame the monster and bring him to Eurystheus; the latter, as had been the case with the Erymantheian boar, was so terrified that he hid himself in his bronze pithos.

The Apples of Hesperides

The final demand made by Eurystheus was that Herakles should bring him the golden apples of Hesperides. These were to be found in the garden of the gods, in the far West, where the Hesperides – the daughters of Night – had their home. The apples were guarded by Ladon, a serpent with one hundred heads. Following instructions from Nereus, Herakles travelled from Africa to Asia and from there to the Caucasus where he set Prometheus free. The latter, to thank him, advised him to ask for help from his brother, Atlas, who lived next to the garden and held up the sky in his hands. The Titan consented to help Herakles, thus finding an opportunity to have a rest from the weight that he had been supporting. He handed him the sky and then set off to take the apples. Thanks to the help of the Hesperides, who sent Ladon to sleep, Atlas picked three golden apples and brought them to Herakles. However, not wishing to take back the great burden, he suggested that Herakles should remain holding the sky and that he instead would go to Eurystheus. Herakles pretended to agree and asked him to hold the sky for just a short moment until he could put something soft on his shoulders to make things more comfortable. Thus, he managed to escape, having handed the burden back to Atlas.

Herakles and Antaios.

Lesser tasks

At the same time as the great labours, and while he was trying to carry out what had been ordered, Herakles accomplished other deeds and had other adventures. One of these was the skirmish with the **Centaurs** on his way to capture the Keryneian hind. The cause of the incident was the wine which he had drunk with the centaur Pholos one evening, as his guest. Its aroma lured the other centaurs which, also wishing to drink, arrived with their weapons. Herakles killed most of them and by mistake mortally wounded Cheiron.

In Pelion, while on his way to collect the Apples of the Hesperides, he met **Kyknos**, son of Ares, who waited in ambush for pilgrims to Delphi, robbed them and cut off their heads in order to build a temple with their skulls. His duel with Herakles, however, was his last. When Ares saw that his son was dead, he moved against Herakles. The latter,

Herakles and Kyknos

however, with the help of Athena, even managed to wound the god of war. On the same mission, passing through Libya, he met the giant **Antaios**, son of Poseidon and Gaia who was invincible because he drew off his strength from the earth. As he used to

*When Herakles wounded the centaur Cheiron by mistake, the latter used a plant called the "Great Centaurion" (***Centaurea mixta***) to treat the wound but was unsuccessful. The same plant is called "Cheironias" or "The blood of Herakles".*

invite all strangers to wrestle with him, he fought with Herakles who managed to beat him by lifting him up completely and thus severing his connection with the source of his power. He also passed through Egypt, where **Busiris** was king and used to seize passers-by and sacrifice them on the altar of Zeus at Memphis. When he was about to sacrifice Herakles, the latter rose up and killed Busiris and his men on the altar instead. In Ethiopia he killed king **Imathion**, son of Eos, who would not let him pass through his country. On his quest for the apples, Herakles went to Caucasus where he freed **Prometheus** and later on to Macedonia, where he killed king **Lykaon** who challenged him

Herakles killed Iphitos in order to take revenge on his father Eurytos who would not give him his daughter Iole for a wife. When a fit of madness overcame him, he went to the oracle at Delphi to ask how he might be cured of the sickness. Since he was still stained by the murder of Iphitos, the oracle refused to answer him and Herakles, enraged, stole the tripod of the oracle. Only Zeus, by throwing his thunderbolt, could interrupt the contest with Apollo which ensued.

Herakles prepares to attack Alkyon while he is sleeping.

to a duel. Finally, he killed **Alkyon** who lived in Corinth and tried to steal the cattle of Geryon, with a huge rock. In addition to the small deeds that accompanied the larger labours, Herakles also carried out some very brave acts, such as that which provoked the campaign against **Troy**. Laomedon, son of Troos, was king of Troy, but he drew the anger of Poseidon because he did not thank the god for building the walls of the city. Thus Poseidon sent a sea-monster to ravage the land. Near to panic, Laomedon was informed by the oracle at Delphi that he must sacrifice a child. When the lot fell on his own daughter, Hesione, Laomedon promised that whoever killed the monster would receive the immortal horses which had been a gift of Zeus to his father as a reward. Herakles succeeded, but the king did not keep his promise, so the hero, with the help of a few brave warriors, organized a campaign against Troy in which he subsequently killed Laomedon.

Herakles shoots the centaur Nessos.

The Deification of Herakles

In addition to Megara, Herakles also took Deianeira, sister of Meleager, as his wife, as he had promised him when he met him in Hades. In order to marry her he had to fight a duel with Acheloos, to whom she had been promised by her father Oineas, king of Kalydon. They had four sons, Hyllos, Ktesippos, Glinos and Oneites. When one day they wanted to travel to Tiryns, they had to cross the river Euenos and in order to do this Herakles sought help for Deianeira from the centaur Nessos. When in the midst of transporting her across the river Nessos attempted to rape her, Herakles killed him. The centaur, shortly before he died, told

Deianeira to collect his blood and to use it as a philtre every time another woman tried to claim her husband. Once, when Eurytos, king of Oichalia, announced that he would marry his daughter Iole to whoever could beat him with a bow and arrow, Herakles took part in the contest and won. However, Eurytos did not keep his promise and Herakles returned to Tiryns, where later on in a fit of madness he took his revenge on Eurytos by killing his son, Iphitos. He also stole the tripod of the oracle at Delphi in a fit of madness, provoking a fierce confrontation with Apollo which was resolved by the intervention of Zeus. In order to be released from his madness and atone for the slaying, in accordance with a prophecy, Herakles had to serve Omphale, the queen of Lydia. After fulfilling this duty, during which he performed a number of other deeds, he returned to Greece, conquered Oichalia and killed Eurytos and his children – all except for Iole, whom many believed he loved. When subsequently he prepared a magnificent sacrifice of thanks to Zeus, he wore the cloak which Deianeira had sent him. She, however, had dipped it in the magic philtre that Nessos had given her, believing that her husband was abandoning her for Iole. He had hardly put on the cloak and drew near to the fire, when it began to stick to him and terrible pains afflicted his whole body. He asked to be taken to the peak of Oitis and be burned there on a pyre. When his son Hyllos refused to light the fire, Herakles asked this favour from Philoctetes, a passer-by. As soon as the fire began to blaze, thunder and lightning could be heard, and a cloud covered the pyre. No trace of the body of Herakles remained, because the cloud bore him to Olympos where he found that place which belonged to him – alongside the gods. There, he became friends with Hera and married Hebe, the goddess of youth.

Athena leads Herakles to Olympos.

Kadmos

The founder of Thebes and the 'Spartans'

Kadmos was the son of Agenor, king of Phoenicia, and Telephassa, and the brother of Phoenix, Kilix and Europa. When Zeus, in the form of a bull, tricked and abducted Europa, Agenor sent his sons to find her. The brothers went their separate ways and Kadmos went to Greece where, after many wanderings, he arrived at the oracle in Delphi. There he was told that he should stop his search and instead follow a cow. When it stopped, he should found a city and reside there. Thus he came to found Thebes and decided to sacrifice the cow to Athena. When however he sent his comrades to bring water from a spring, they were terrified by the monstrous snake guarding it. Kadmos was angry and crushed the snake, which was an offspring of the god Ares himself. Athena advised Kadmos to scatter the teeth of the snake and these sprouted to produce the 'Spartans', an armed race which was totally destroyed in internecine strife except for five individuals who became the founders of the Kadmeia. To achieve his atonement, Zeus set Kadmos to serve Ares.

Harmonia and the sons of Kadmos

After having served Ares, Kadmos became king of Thebes and married Harmonia, daughter of Ares and Aphrodite. All of the gods were present at their magnificent wedding and gave the couple rich gifts. Kadmos gave his bride a necklace wrought by Hephaestos himself and the Graces wove a shimmering robe for her. They had five children: Semele, Ino, Agaue, Autonoe and Polydoros. Semele eventually became the mother of a god, Dionysos; but she was unlucky. She managed to give birth, but through intervention by Hera she was burned to death by the brilliance of Zeus, when she demanded that he appear before her in all his glory. Ino became the second wife of king Athamas of Orchomenos and produced Learchos and Melikertes, but because she had nourished the new-born Dionysos, Hera instilled such a madness in both her and her husband that they killed their own children. Agaue became queen of

Thebes after marrying Echion, one of the Spartans. However, since she had said bad things about Semele, Dionysos took his revenge by making her a maenad and leading her, in her ecstasy, to kill her son Pentheus. Autonoe married Aristaios, son of Apollo. Together they produced Aktaeon, the wonderful hunter and companion of Artemis who set her dogs to tear him limb from limb when he desired to see her naked. Lastly, Polydoros became king of Thebes when his parents went to Illyria.

With his wife Nykteida he had a son, Labdakos, who became the head of the other great family of Boeotia, the Labdakids. Kadmos and Harmonia reached old age as rulers in Illyria. He could never forget that

Hounds tear apart Aktaeon, the grandson of Kadmos.

he had been the slayer of a divine snake, and thus asked the gods to transform him and his wife into benevolent snakes.

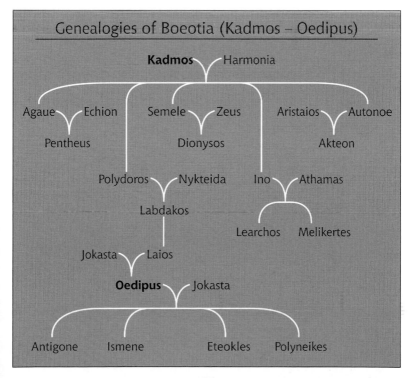

Genealogies of Boeotia (Kadmos – Oedipus)

Kadmos ⌣ Harmonia

Agaue ⌣ Echion   Semele ⌣ Zeus   Aristaios ⌣ Autonoe

Pentheus   Dionysos   Akteon

Polydoros ⌣ Nykteida   Ino ⌣ Athamas

Labdakos

Learchos   Melikertes

Jokasta ⌣ Laios

Oedipus ⌣ Jokasta

Antigone   Ismene   Eteokles   Polyneikes

Oedipus

The Labdakids and Oedipus

Labdakos, son of Polydoros and grandson of Kadmos, met the same end as his cousin Pentheus, being torn limb from limb by maenads. His son Laios became king of Thebes and married Jokasta, sister of Creon and daughter of Manoikeus. Since the oracle at Delphi had warned Laios that, if he had a child, the latter would kill him and marry his own mother, Laios had no relations with his wife except for one occasion when he was drunk; he lay with her and subsequently a boy was born. Terrified, he pierced the ankles of the infant, put gold links in them and joined the feet together, then gave him to a shepherd to abandon him on mount Kithairon, in the hope that he would not survive because of hunger or attack by wild animals. The shepherd

The shepherd takes the baby Oedipus to Kithairon.

took the child to the mountain, but feeling sorry for him gave him to some shepherds of king Polybos of Corinth. They took him to queen Merope who received him joyfully because she had no children of her own. They called him Oedipus, which means 'the one with swollen feet', and raised him in the palace as their own. One day, when Oedipus was amusing himself in the company of his friends, one of them became drunk and revealed to him that he was the adopted son of the royal couple. Subsequently, since his parents would not answer his questions, he went to the oracle at Delphi which revealed to him that he would kill his father and marry his mother. Thinking therefore that his parents were Polybos and Merope, he decided not to return to Corinth. One day, on his wanderings, he came upon Laios and his entourage who had gone to Delphi to find out what had become of his son. When they demanded that he step aside so that the king could pass, he refused. The royal chariot continued on its way and ran over the feet of Oedipus. The latter was very angry and killed the king's herald. Then Laios hit Oedipus on the head with his scepter, whereby Oedipus in his rage, killed the king and his companions, except for one who returned to Thebes and related what had happened. Thus,

Creon, the brother of Jokasta, became king of Thebes. A terrible monster now appeared with the head of a woman and body of a lion. This was the Sphinx and it posed the following riddle; what is it that has two legs, four legs, and three legs? Whosoever could not find the answer was killed, and Thebes passed through difficult times. Then Creon announced that whoever could solve the riddle would become king and marry Jokasta. The only one to give the right answer was Oedipus, who said that the creature described by the Sphinx was Man himself. Thus he became king of Thebes and married his mother, Jokasta.

King of Thebes

As king of Thebes and husband of Jokasta, Oedipus produced four children – Antigone, Ismene, Eteokles and Polyneikes. When on one occasion a plague broke out in the city, Oedipus sent Creon to Delphi to find out what was happening. The answer was that the murderer of Laios had to be found. When, in spite of the threats issued, nobody came forward to admit responsibility, Oedipus turned to the seer Teiresias who after much persuasion revealed the truth: the murderer of Laios was Oedipus himself. The latter, believing that Creon had engineered this apportioning of guilt, condemned his brother-in-law to death. However, when Jokasta gave him details of the king's death, Oedipus realized that he himself had been the murderer. At the same time, it was

Oedipus and the Sphinx, Jean Auguste-Dominique Ingres, 1808, Paris, Louvre.

The blind seer Teiresias is led by a boy to Oedipus (?) who seeks to learn the truth.

announced that Polybos had died and Oedipus could take power in Corinth. When he said that he was afraid to go to his own country lest the prophecy that he would marry his own mother might come true, the shepherd appeared and revealed that he was the adopted son of the royal couple of Corinth. Terrified, Oedipus questioned the old shepherd from Kithairon and the tragic truth was out: he had killed his father and married his own mother. Hearing the terrible news, Jokasta hanged herself, and Oedipus blinded himself with the pins from her robe.

Asylum and death in Athens

Blind and driven out, with his daughter Antigone as his only companion, he left Thebes and went to Athens where he sought asylum from its king, Theseus, with the promise that he would bring great good to the city. In the meantime Ismene arrived and informed him of developments in Thebes: his two sons, Polyneikes and Eteokles had fought for power and the younger had driven out Polyneikes who had fled to Argos. There he had married the daughter of king Adrastos and began to prepare for the campaign 'Seven Against Thebes', against his own city. At the same time, Creon began to look for Oedipus to bring him back so that, when he died, the curses of Laios would fall upon his tomb and the city would be spared. After the intervention of Theseus, Oedipus was pardoned by Creon and chased away Polyneikes who came to ask him to help him seize power. Shortly before his end he called Theseus and in order to repay the kindness that he had shown him, entrusted to him a secret with which Athens would be delivered from eventual attack by Thebes. Then the earth opened, and Oedipus was swallowed up at a location known only to Theseus.

The children of Oedipus

Four children were born out of the incestuous relationship of Oedipus with Jokasta: Antigone, Ismene, Polyneikes and Eteokles. After the tragic revelation of the truth, the self-inflicted blinding and exile of Oedipus from Thebes, Eteokles – although he was the youngest – seized power from his brother. Thus Polyneikes fled to Argos, where he married the daughter of king Adrastos and had a son, Thersander, who later became king of Thebes. In Argos, Polyneikes organized the campaign of 'Seven Against Thebes', which was not only fruitless, but also cost the lives of the two brothers who were killed in a duel. Creon, as the man of power now that Eteokles was dead, ordered the latter, as king, to be buried, but Polyneikes as a traitor to remain unburied outside the walls of the city. Antigone, who could not accept this impiety against her brother, undertook to bury the body secretely with the help of Ismene.

Creon punished her for this act by having her walled up alive. Later on Creon, told by the seer Teiresias of portents sent by the gods, wanted to release her but found that she had hanged herself with a sheet in the very place that he had imprisoned her. They say that Ismene met her end during the siege of Thebes; the fierce Tydeas, one of the 'Seven' besiegers, butchered her in the temple of Athena where he found her together with her lover Periklymenos, son of Poseidon.

Tydeas kills Ismene.

Jason

His descent

When Thessaly was still known as Aeolis, there ruled there a king, Aeolos, the son of Hellen and the nymph Ortheis. With Enaréti he produced Kretheus, Athamas, Sisyphos, Salmoneus and Perieres. Of these sons, the last three left Thessaly and became kings in cities of the Peloponnese. Athamas married Nefeli first of all and fathered Phrixos and Helle, and then he married Ino, daughter of Kadmos, who bore him Learchos and Melikertes.

Kretheus married his own niece, Tyro, the daughter of his arrogant brother Salmoneus. They had three sons: Aeson, Amythaon and Pheres. Meanwhile Tyro, shortly before she married Kretheus, had lain with Poseidon and had secretly born two sons; as soon as they were delivered, she put them into a boat and cast it adrift in the river. When a horse-herder found them, he saved them and called them Pelias and Neleas. Later, when Tyro chanced to hear the story from the shepherd, she recognized them and took them back. Pelias followed Kretheus on the throne of Iolchos, although the legitimate heir was the first-born son of Kretheus, Aeson. The latter, supplanted, had in the meantime married Polymela and produced Jason; he left Iolchos and handed over his son to the centaur Cheiron in Pelion. When Jason was twenty years of age, a brave and well-

As **Ino** did not like her husband's children, **Phrixos** and Helle, she devised the following plan: together with the women of Thessaly, she rendered the seed for sowing useless, so that it would not bear any fruit in the following year. Then she bribed the ambassadors of Athamas to Delphi so that they would bring a false prophecy, according to which Phrixos should be sacrificed to Zeus. When all was then prepared for the sacrifice, Nefeli appeared, snatched her son and lifted him and his sister onto the back of a ram with a golden fleece which Hermes had given to her. During the journey that followed, Helle fell off and drowned in the sea which is called the Hellespont, while Phrixos reached Colchis where king Aeëtes ruled. He sacrificed the ram to Zeus, presented the Golden Fleece to the king and married his daughter, Chalkiope.

trained warrior, he decided to return to Iolchos and claim the throne from Pelias. Arriving at a time when they were preparing a sacrifice, his beauty drew wonder from the king but also caused him panic, for he immediately noticed that he was wearing only one sandal. A prophecy had forewarned Pelias that he would lose his power to a man who only wore one sandal. Jason had lost a sandal on the way, when an old woman, who was actually none other than Hera herself in transformation, made him cross a swollen river. Pelias at once realized the danger of his situation and asserted that he had no objection to giving him his throne, provided that the young man would bring him the Golden Fleece from Colchis.

The Argonauts and the Argo.

The voyage of the Argonauts

Faced with the challenge issued by Pelias, Jason immediately began to organize an expedition to Colchis. Under instructions from Athena he built the 'Argo', a large and fast ship and with the exhortations of Hera he gathered together the most illustrious and brave warriors from all the areas of Greece: Herakles with Hylas, the father of Achilles, Peleas, father of Ajax, Telamon, Laertes, who was the father of Odysseus, and his grandfather Autolykos, Deucalion father of Idomeneus, Melegros, the Dioscorides Kastor and Polydeuces, the Apharetides Idas and Lynkeas, Akastos son of Pelias, Argos the builder of the Argo, Orpheus, the seers Idmonas and Mopsos, and many others. When the Argo was ready and the Argonauts had gathered, the seer Mopsos, seeing that the omens were favourable, suggested that they set off. Their first port of call was **Lemnos**. It was ruled by Hypsipyle and inhabited only by women. They had all killed their own husbands because they had foresaken them and only gone with concubines. The reason that they had been abandoned was because they imparted an unbearable stench which had been inflicted on them by Aphrodite because they had not paid her honour. In order to avoid a clash with them and to be able to stop on the island, the Argonauts promised that they would lay with them. Thus, Jason produced two sons with Hypsipyle, Euenos and Nevrophonos. The next stops were **the Island of Chryse** and **Samothrace** on the way to **Troy** where Herakles freed Hesione, the daughter of king Laomedon who was about to be sacrificed, and killed the sea monster which was tormenting the

city. Thereafter the Argonauts passed through the Hellespont and arrived at Kyzikos in the south of the Propontis. It was inhabited by the Doliones, whose king was **Kyzikos**. In spite of the fact that they were given hospitality and departed in contentment, when they had to return to the harbour because of bad weather the Doliones did not recognize them again because of the darkness of the night and attacked them. A wild confrontation ensued in which Jason killed the king himself and it was only with the first light of day that they realized their folly, which had been caused by a misunderstanding. They buried their dead, organized games and founded a temple dedicated to the mother of the gods, Rhea. Their next port of call was

Arganthoneio in Propontis whence they departed, unwillingly leaving Herakles behind; he had lost

his way in the forest looking for his friend Hylas whom a nymph had taken away with her. The journey continued to the land of the seer **Phineas**. This seer, who had misused his prophetic talent, lived there blind and punished by Zeus so that every time he tried to eat the Harpies would snatch his food. When the Argonauts Kalaïs and Zetes chased away the monsters and the seer had been rescued he, in return, gave them useful information for their journey and in particular told them how they could pass the **Symplegades**, the rocks which drew apart and clashed together with such terrible speed and broke up ships. Following his advice, they first released a dove, and when it managed to pass them with the loss of only a few feathers from its tail, they passed through with the Argo, which was damaged only lightly on its stern. Thus they arrived successfully in the Black Sea and after passing **the land of the Mariandynoi**, where the seer Idmonas and the helmsman Tiphys lost their lives, they turned toward **Colchis.**

After Lemnos the Argonauts stopped on the Island of Chryse where they raised an altar to Athena Chryse.

The Argonauts in Colchis

Aeëtes, son of Helios and the Okeanida Perse, was king of Colchis. With Eidyia he produced Medea and Chalkiope and with Eurylyte he produced Apsyrtos. Since Aeëtes had learned from a prophecy that he would only keep his throne as long as the golden fleece stayed in the forest of Ares, he said that he would give Jason the throne when he had carried out a number of labours, hoping thus to destroy him. He ordered him to yoke two bulls - which spouted flames from their mouths and had bronze claws - to plough, sow the teeth of a snake and then defeat the giants which would spring up from them. With the help of Medea, who was a witch and in the meantime had fallen in love with him, Jason carried out this mission. Seeing however that Aeëtes was going to set him another task, Medea herself took him to the forest of Ares, sent the dragon which guarded the golden fleece to sleep and made it easy for her lover to snatch

According to one account Jason, in order to defeat the dragon with the impregnable skin, entered its stomach with the help of Athena and killed it from within.

it. Thus the Argonauts, together with Medea as Jason had promised her, embarked on board the Argo once more and secretly left Colchis.

*Medea is said to have sent the dragon to sleep with **Colchicum**, a poisonous plant.*

Medea poisons the dragon, and Jason steals the golden fleece.

The witch Circe.

The return journey

With the trophy of victory and remembering that the seer Phineas had advised them not to return by the same route, they sailed towards the north-west of the Black Sea and from there followed the course of the river Istron. They were soon confronted by the Colchians, who had pursued them on the orders of Aeëtes. In the closely-fought battle Apsyrtos, the brother of Medea, was killed. On the other hand, some said that during the pursuit by Aeëtes, Medea herself cut her brother into pieces and threw them into the sea to slow down her father, who stopped in order to pick them up. They had just entered the Adriatic and were heading for Kerkyra when a strong wind blew them back, a sign that they would have to be cleansed of the slaughter of Apsyrtos. The Argo herself, which had the power to speak, told them that they would have to go to Circe, sister of Aeëtes, who lived on the island called Aeaea, somewhere on the western shores of Italy. Sailing down the Eridanos and the river Rodanos they came to the Tyrrhenian Sea and turned south. They passed the little islands of the Stichades and Aethalia, and came to Aeaea where they were cleansed by Circe and then proceeded on towards Anthemoessa, home of the Sirens. Thanks to Orpheus, they were able to sail past these sorceresses who could disorientate sailors with their melodies; he played his lyre and drowned out the song. Thereafter they passed Scylla and Charybdis and with the help of Hera and Thetis through the Clashing Rocks, moving cliffs which crushed ships. Then they went to the island of the Phaeacians where Jason married Medea, to the disappointment of the Colchians who had come to take her back. Continuing southwards, shortly before they arrived at the Peloponnese a strong wind blew up which after nine days threw them onto the northern

In order to destroy the bronze giant **Talos**, who circled Crete three times every day to stop ships from anchoring on the island, Medea practiced the following deception: knowing that his life depended on a vein which ran to his ankle and was closed off with a bronze nail, she told him that in order to become immortal he would have to remove it. Thus Talos drew out the nail, his blood flowed out and he fell down dead.

shore of Africa. There the Argo stuck fast in the sand and the Argonauts, having lost hope, sought help from the gods; interpreting the signs, they came to the conclusion that they would have to lift the Argo with their own arms and cross the desert. They did this, and after twelve days arrived at Lake Tritonis, whence with the help of the god Triton, they found a channel to the sea. In order to sail past Crete, they had to destroy the giant Talos; after this had been accomplished they passed Anaphi and finally arrived at Iolchos.

Medea stabs her children to death.

Medea, Eugene Delacroix, 1862.

Jason and Medea in Iolchos

When Jason returned to Iolchos with the golden fleece, he was informed that not only did Pelias have no intention of handing power to him as promised, but that he had killed all his family. Full of anger, he began to plan a method of revenge with the Argonauts. Then Medea appeared and said that she would undertake to destroy the king using her deadly magic philtres. She transformed herself into a priestess of Artemis, hid her lethal herbs inside a little statue of the goddess and went to the palace, announcing that she had been sent by Artemis to restore youth to the pious king. She managed to convince him and set his own daughters to kill him, saying that this was simply the first phase of the procedure. The Argonauts then arrived and as soon as the daughters of Pelias saw them they realized that they had been tricked and wanted to kill themselves.

Jason not only prevented them from doing so but withdrew from any exercise of power which he handed to Akastos, the son of Pelias. Then he took Medea and they left for Corinth where they stayed in the palace of Creon. When Jason fell in love with Glauke, the daughter of the king, and decided to marry her, Medea, whom they had ordered to leave the palace, wanted to take revenge on her husband. Thus she sent the bride a wedding present: a dress and a crown which she had previously smeared with magic ointment. When the girl put them on, she was engulfed in flames and burnt to death along with her father, who tried to save her. Thereafter, having killed her two children, Medea went to Athens where she married king Aegeus and bore him a son.

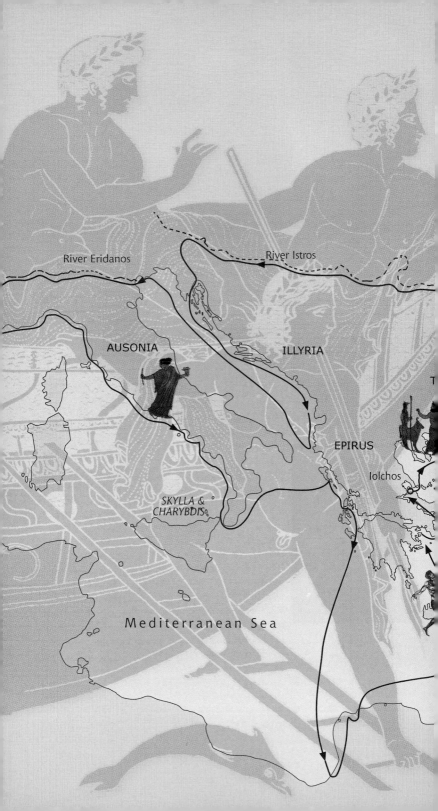

River Eridanos

River Istros

AUSONIA

ILLYRIA

EPIRUS

T

Iolchos

SKYLLA &
CHARYBDIS

Mediterranean Sea

The voyage of the Argonauts

Euxine Sea
(Black Sea)

COLCHIS

Mariandynoi

Amazons

Cyzicus

PAPHLAGONIA

PHRYGIA

CYPRUS

RETE

The Kalydonian Boar. 590/580 B.C. Museum of Delphi.

Meleager

In Aetolia there were two rival cities, Kalydon and Pleuron, founded by the sons of the same name of Aetolos. Later, Oineas ruled in Kalydon; he had a wife, Althaea and a son, Meleager. Once, when he forgot to sacrifice to Artemis, the goddess punished him by sending a boar which devoured everything and devastated the royal property. In order to combat the destruction, Meleager invited all the warriors who so desired to take part in a hunt for the boar and whoever killed it would receive its hide as a reward. The heroes gathered, some from neighbouring Pleuron where the Kuretes ruled; among them was the brother of Althaea. Also present were Kastor and Polydeuces from Sparta, Idas and Lynkeas from Messenia, Amphiaraos from Argos, Peleas, Jason and Mopsos from Thessaly, Theseus from Athens, Telamon from Salamis, Atalanta – a woman from Arkadia - and many others. The hunt began and many were killed, either by the boar itself or by various obstacles. Finally the uncle of Meleager hit the boar and he himself finished it off. Since the two of them believed that they had achieved the impossible, each claimed the hide and as a result a fierce battle began between the inhabitants of the two rival cities. During the fight Meleager, whether by design or not, killed his uncle. When the news of the loss of her brother reached the ears of Althaea, she asked the gods to send her son to the Underworld. Meleager heard of his mother's curse, became angry and left the battle. Thus the Kuretes were then

*According to another account the first one to hit the boar was **Atalanta**. When he had finished it off, Meleager, having fallen in love with her, wanted to give her the hide. The men, and in particular his uncle, were insulted and claimed the trophy, taking it from her. Then Meleager grew angry and, defending her, killed them.*

able to proceed to the storming of Kalydon. At this critical hour all began to implore the brave fighter to come back and help the city but only his wife, Kleopatra, was able to persuade him. So Meleager came back into the battle and saved Kalydon, but as a result of Althaea's curse he lost his life.

Bellerophon

The first king of Corinth, before the city was thus named, was clever, crafty Sisyphos. His son Glaukos, together with Eurynome, daughter of Nisos of Megara, produced Bellerophon, who was really the son of Poseidon. At the time when he, as heir, took over power, Proitos was king in Argos, and his wife was Anteia. At some stage Anteia - or Stheneboia - who was the daughter of Iobates king of Lycia, fell in love with Bellerophon; her feelings were not returned. Therefore, the crafty woman, fearing that he might denounce her to her husband, twisted the facts and told Proitos that Bellerophon had molested her. Proitos wanted to punish him without appearing to do so; therefore he sent him to his father-in-law, ostensibly to bring him an important message. The message was none other than that Iobates was to find some way to kill the handsome warrior. So when the king of Lycia received the message he decided to get rid of him by sending him on some impossible missions. The first of

The "Chimaera of Arezzo". 5th century B.C. Archaeological Museum, Florence.

these was to kill the Chimaera, which was devouring the flocks in Lycia.
Bellerophon however, in view of the fact that he had received the winged horse Pegasos from his father Poseidon as a gift, did not experience any difficulty. He flew high on his horse and killed the Chimaera with an arrow. Thereafter he defeated the Solymoi, a race hostile to Iobates, and the Amazons. When Iobates realized that he was not dealing with an ordinary man, and since he had no other difficult mission to give him, he married him to his daughter Cassandra and gave him some of the power in Lycia.
Despite his victories and his glorious life,

The terrible **Chimaera** was the offspring of Typhoon with Echidna. Her siblings were the monstrous hound Orthos, Cerberus the guardian of Hades, the Lernaian Hydra, Scylla, the dragon which guarded the Apples of the Hesperides, the dragon which guarded the golden fleece, the Sphinx, the Nemean lion and the eagle which devoured the liver of Prometheus. The Chimaera had the head of a lion, the body of a goat and a tail with a snake's head at its tip.

Bellerophon's demise was sad: when he decided to fly on Pegasos to Olympos, the horse hurled him to earth, as a punishment for his arrogance.

Pelops

Although his descent was from far-off Lydia, Pelops was destined to be included in the mythical genealogy of Elis. He was the son of Tantalos and Dione, daughter of Atlas. Tantalos, as a son of Zeus and a pious man, had such good relations with the gods that he was judged worthy to partake of a meal on Olympos. In order to reciprocate in some way he invited the gods and in order to please them he slaughtered his son Pelops and offered him to them. They were very angry and for this reason they brought Pelops back to life and sent Tantalos to Hades, condemning him to eternal hunger and thirst.

At some stage Pelops fell in love with Hippodameia, the daughter of Oinomaos, king of Elis and Pisa. The latter, a son of Ares, had received a prophecy that he would die as soon as Hippodameia married. In order to prevent the marriage of his daughter therefore, he announced that she would be given to the man who won a chariot race with him. His weapons - by which he never lost a race -were actually his swift horses, a gift from his father Ares, and the condition that he set was that every candidate for bridegroom would have to have Hippodameia in the chariot with him. Thus the girl's beauty would cause a distraction and Oinomaos would surely win. Under these preconditions and with the help of his charioteer Myrtilos, son of Hermes, he beat all the ambitious suitors, killed them and kept their heads in a pile in his palace. Pelops, who loved Hippodameia very much, realized that in order to win he would have to form a conspiracy with Myrtilos. Together they agreed that the charioteer would destabilize the chariot of Oinomaos by

Not only Oinomaos had divine horses. Poseidon appeared to Pelops one evening, riding on a hippocamp, and gave him horses which were just as swift and strong as those of Oinomaos.

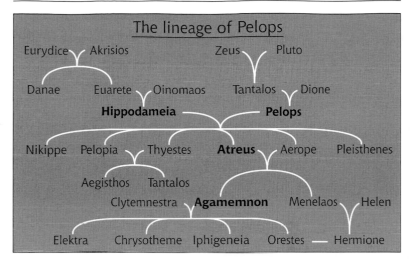

The lineage of Pelops

Eurydice — Akrisios Zeus — Pluto

Danae Euarete — Oinomaos Tantalos — Dione

Hippodameia — **Pelops**

Nikippe Pelopia — Thyestes **Atreus** — Aerope Pleisthenes

Aegisthos Tantalos

Clytemnestra **Agamemnon** Menelaos — Helen

Elektra Chrysotheme Iphigeneia Orestes — Hermione

replacing the bolts which connected the wheels to the axle with waxen ones; as a reward he would have one night with his beloved Hippodameia. Thus Oinomaos was killed, but he realized the treachery of Myrtilos and cursed him so that he would find death at the hands of Pelops himself. The victorious Pelops, together with Hippodameia and the charioteer Myrtilos, returned to the palace. On the way however, Myrtilos tried to rape Hippodameia and Pelops took the opportunity to get rid of him by throwing him into the sea. Despite a curse uttered by Myrtilos, Pelops became king of Elis and Pisa and later on managed to rule over - and give his name to - all of the Peloponnese.

The accursed tribe of the Atreids

The power of the dynasty of Pelops in the Peloponnese began to increase when the other great dynasty, that of the Perseids, withdrew from centre stage. Of the children of Perseus there remained Sthenelos who married Nikippe, one of the daughters of Pelops. He gave some of his power to his brothers-in-law, Atreus and Thyestes, who were to extend it in particular after the death of the only son of Sthenelos, Eurystheus. Even though the two sons of Pelops conspired against their half-brother Chrysippos and killed him, they subsequently quarrelled with each other for power. Finally, with the assistance of Zeus, Atreus won; when he discovered that his brother had had secret relations with his wife Aerope, he invited him to dinner and fed him with his own children. Thyestes, following the advice of a prophecy, then fathered Aegisthus on his own daughter Pelopia. Aegisthus later killed Atreus and ascended to the throne of his father, Thyestes. Then the children of Atreus, Agamemnon and Menelaos, fled to Sparta which was ruled by king Tyndareus and his wife Leda, with their children the Dioskouroi, Helen, and Clytemnestra. Subsequently the king himself married Agamemnon to Clytemnestra who bore him three children – Iphigeneia, Elektra and Orestes – and Menelaos to Helen, who bore Hermione. He also helped Agamemnon to regain power at Mycenae, while Menelaos inherited his power at Sparta. Overshadowed however by the weight of the curses of Pelops, Thyestes and Myrtilos, life in the two kingdoms underwent dramatic developments within the framework of the Trojan War.

Perseus

After many contests the twin brothers Akrisios and Proitos shared power as follows: Proitos became king of Tiryns and Akrisios king of Argos. The latter married Eurydice and they had two daughters, Danäe and Euarete, who latter married Oinomaos. As he had received a prophecy that his grandson would kill him, he locked Danäe away in a cellar so that she could not have relations with any man. She was beautiful, however, and Zeus desired her, so he entered her room in the form of a golden shower of rain and lay with her. Danäe bore Perseus, and when Akrisios found out, he put his daughter and her baby into a box and threw it into the sea. On Serifos a fisherman, Diktys, found the box and looked after mother and baby. The king of the island at that time was Polydektes who subsequently wanted to take Danäe to wife. On one occasion he organized a supper party to which the invited guests were each to bring a horse as a gift, Perseus boasted that he could bring the head of the Gorgon. The king ordered him to do this, saying that if he did not succeed he would take Danäe as his wife. Now, Perseus had to find a solution. While in this difficult position Hermes appeared to him and said that together with Athena he would help him to take the head of Medusa, the only one of the Gorgons that was mortal. All that was needed was the

According to Hesiod, the **Gorgons**, daughters of Phorkys and Keto, lived further away than the Graies, towards the west and beyond the sky. There were three of them: Stheno, Euryale, and Medusa. The first two were ageless and immortal, while Medusa was mortal. They had golden wings, bronze arms, tusks, and snakes grew out of their heads. Whoever gazed on their terrible face would be turned to stone. After cutting off the head of Medusa, Perseus gave her face to Athena who placed it in the middle of her shield and always carried it with her.

right equipment: a cap to make him invisible, winged sandals so that he would not have to tread on the ground, and a sack in which to put the head. This should be done without gazing upon it, otherwise he would be turned to stone. After obtaining the equipment from the nymphs Perseus, assisted by the gods, managed to decapltate Medusa, from whose neck there sprang Pegasos, the winged horse, and Chrysaor, the warrior with the golden sword.

With the trophy in the sack, Perseus set off for Serifos. However, while passing through Ethiopia he noticed a most beautiful girl tied to a rock. This was **Andromeda**, daughter of Kepheus and Kassiope, who in order to fulfill a prophecy had been destined as food for the sea monster which was ravaging the land, They said that Poseidon had sent the monster to punish Kassiope who had boasted that her daughter was more beautiful than any of the Nereids. Perseus immediately fell in love with the girl, killed the monster, and freed her. When however her father and her brother refused to give her to him for his wife, he drew the head of the Medusa out of the sack and turned them to stone.

The lineage of Perseus

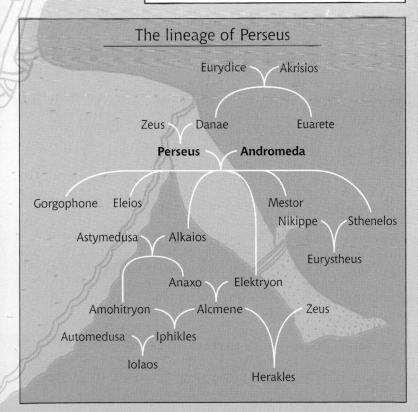

107

THE TROJAN WAR

THE TROJAN WAR

All for a woman called Helen...

We all know that the motive for the Trojan War was the kidnapping of the beautiful Helen by Paris. The real reason however, was the increase of the earth's population; in order to limit it Zeus decided to start a number of wars.

The story of the war does not begin with the 'abduction' of Helen, but slightly earlier – that is, with the marriage of Peleus and Thetis. The latter, a beautiful Nereid, had excited the passion of two of the great gods, Zeus and Poseidon. However, Themis –the goddess of justice – warned them that whoever married her would produce a son who would become more powerful than himself. Thus the two gods cooled their amorous desires and decided to marry off Thetis to Peleus, the king of Pelion and son of Ajax who ruled in Aegina. One night, Peleus went down to the seashore, where the Nereid and her friends were playing, and tried to possess her. Being a goddess, she began to transform herself, first into a snake, then a dragon, and then a lion to escape him. Peleus however, held her tightly until finally she became his. The wedding took place immediately and all the gods were invited to the glittering ceremony; they brought wonderful gifts. The only goddess not to be invited was Eris, goddess of discord; to get her revenge for the insult she appeared at the feast bearing a golden apple for the most beautiful goddess present. When Hera, Athena and Aphrodite all claimed the apple,

According to some, in order to solve the problem of the overpopulation of the earth, Zeus took counsel with Themis and according to others with Momos, the son of Night, who suggested that he produce Helen and that he marry Peleus to Thetis, creating the prerequisites for a great war.
The marriage of Peleus and Thetis. Edward Burne-Jones (1833-98) City Museum and Art Gallery, Birmingham.

Paris lived as a shepherd in the mountains of Troy, because before Hekabe bore him she had a dream that the child would destroy Troy. Therefore Priam, who had inherited the city from his father Laomedon and had just rebuilt it after it had been besieged by Herakles, gave the infant to a shepherd for him to kill it. The shepherd however took pity on the baby and undertook his upbringing. Thus Paris grew up, became handsome and brave and later on Priam acknowledged him as his son. While he was still a shepherd, Hermes brought the goddesses to him and explained the orders of Zeus.

Zeus set Paris, son of Priam king of Troy, as a judge and ordered Hermes to bring them to him. As soon as they arrived before Paris, they began to promise things: Athena promised strength, Hera promised power, and Aphrodite the most beautiful woman in the whole world - Helen. Since the latter appeared the more enticing to him, he gave the apple to the goddess of love.

Led by Aphrodite, Paris arrived in Sparta and was given hospitality by the king, Menelaos, and his wife Helen. Aphrodite inflamed Helen with an amorous passion for the stranger, and when nine days later Menelaos was obliged to leave for Crete in order to attend the funeral of his grandfather Katreus, she did not hesitate to abandon the royal palace, her husband and her daughter Hermione and leave for Troy with her lover.

*Beautiful Helen was the daughter of **Zeus and Leda**. The story is as follows: Leda, wife of Tyndareus king of Sparta, was bathing in the Eurotas when she was approached by a swan that was being chased by an eagle. The swan, which was none other than Zeus, lay with the queen who that same evening also slept with her husband. Thus Helen was born, as well as twin boys, Kastor and Polydeukes. It was said that Helen and Polydeukes were the immortal children of Zeus, while Kastor was the mortal son of Tyndareus. Apart from Kastor, Tyndareus also had four more daughters by Leda; the most well-known of these was Clytemnestra. He gave the latter in marriage to Agamemnon, but for Helen, who was the more beautiful, it was not easy to choose a husband. When however he let it be known that he would marry her off, all the rulers in Greece were interested, but finally she chose Menelaos who was the brother of Agamemnon, husband of her sister.*

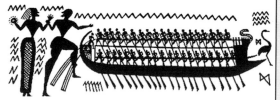

The departure of Helen with Paris. Sketch from a Geometric vase of the 8th century B.C. British Museum, London.

The preparations for the expedition, and its beginning

The flight of Helen, whether voluntary or otherwise, soon reached the ears of Menelaos who returned in great haste to Sparta. When he realized that it was a fact, he hastened to Mycenae and asked his brother Agamemnon to organize an expedition with him to bring Helen back. Agamemnon summoned all the leaders who ten years previously as suitors had put in a claim for Helen and had given their oath to Tyndareus that they would always defend her honour, whatever happened. Along with them, at the suggestions of Nestor, king of Pylos and the seer Calchas, they also invited the wily Odysseus and Achilles, son of Peleus and Thetis.

When all was ready, the Greek forces gathered at Aulis to set off. There however, Agamemnon, hunting in the sacred grove of Artemis, killed one of her deer; the goddess was angered and sent a dead calm, so that the ships could not sail. Then the seer Calchas revealed that in order to be able to leave they would have to sacrifice Iphigeneia, the daughter of Agamemnon. Having

During the first nine years of the campaign the Achaeans were not only busy with waging war. Sometimes they relaxed by playing a game with dice, as is shown in this representation of Achilles and Ajax on a vase dating from the 6th century B.C.

no alternative, he commanded Clytemnestra to send Iphigeneia to Aulis, saying that he intended to marry her to Achilles. At the very moment when Agamemnon raised his sword to sacrifice his own child, Artemis sent him a deer instead, and she took Iphigeneia in a cloud and brought her

The sacrifice of Iphigeneia. Wall-painting based on a lost work of Timanthos (4th century B.C.) at Pompeii, 1st century A.D.

As Polyxena and Troilos approach the spring, Achilles prepares to ambush them.

to Tauris, when she made her a priestess. After the sacrifice, favourable winds permitted the Greek ships to set off on their long expedition. Immediately on arrival at their destination, Menelaos and Odysseus undertook to demand that the Trojans return Helen and the treasure that Paris had taken from the palace at Sparta, and the affair would end there. When, however, they received a refusal, the only thing left was to begin the war. During the first nine years of the war nothing in particular happened, except for some expeditions to neighbouring cities and villages to secure supplies of food, and some skirmishes with the Trojans. During this time Achilles killed Troilos, the little son of Priam, when he came out to collect water with his sister Polyxena.

Thetis, in order to make her only son Achilles immortal, placed him in the fire every evening. When however Peleus discovered what she was doing, he was terrified and took the child and sent him to the centaur **Cheiron**, where he was taught medicine and the arts. Thetis, however, knowing that she had not completed the magic spell and that her son, if he went to war, would die, hid him when he was nine years of age on Skyros, in the palace of Lykomedes.

There he married the king's daughter, **Deidameia**, and they produced Neoptolemos. The envoys of the Achaeans found him there dressed in women's clothes in the hope that they would not recognize him and he would escape the war. However, Odysseus found him out and thus Achilles set off for war.

Deidameia bids Achilles farewell.

113

The protagonists in the war

The Achaeans

The leader of the force was **Agamemnon**, king of Mycenae and brother of Menelaos, because of his great military power which enabled him to participate in the war with one hundred ships. The eldest son of Atreus, he had regained the kingdom from his uncle Thyestes with the help of his father-in-law Tyndareus. With his wife Clytemnestra he produced three children – Iphigeneia, Elektra, and Orestes. His wealth, however, was not paralleled by bravery or by good manners. He was to display arrogance on the field of battle and to come into conflict with Achilles; however, in difficult moments he would not lack courage or modesty.

Menelaos, king of Sparta, was the brother of Agamemnon; he organized the Trojan campaign in order to bring back his wife, Helen. Apart from Hermione, who was his daughter by Helen, he had a son, Megapenthes, by a slave-woman. Sixty ships accompanied him to war and while he was certainly courageous, he could not be compared to the greatest warriors on the expedition. Inspired by Hera and Athena, he fought Paris in a duel and defeated him; nor did he hesitate to accept the challenge of a duel with Hektor.

Nestor, son of Neleus and grandson of Poseidon, was the king of Pylos. Advanced in years - aged around seventy-five - this revered leader was the voice of logic and experience at difficult times during the war. The 'man of many wiles',

Odysseus king of Ithaca, came to the war with twelve ships and stood out because of his dexterity with words and deeds. A leading light in matters of war, politics and even deceit and cunning, he came to be appreciated by all because he often found the solution to the most difficult problems. Practical and stoic, brave and under the protection of Athena, he was to suffer adventures for twenty years until he returned to his homeland, his wife Penelope, and his only son, Telemachos.

Ajax the Salaminian, son of king Telamon, went to war with twelve ships. Huge in body and brave, he was the only one, apart from Achilles, to dare to fight Hektor single-handed. An important fighter, but not of the stature of Ajax, was his bastard brother Teukros.

Ajax the Lokrian, grandson of Apollo, was more slightly-built than his namesake, but he stood out for his swiftness of foot and his excellent skills with the javelin.

Achilles was the bravest and the most handsome of the warriors. Even though his mother Thetis, being a goddess, knew that he would die in battle and tried to prevent his participation, he could not in the end avoid it, because all realised that without him they could not achieve victory. He took with him his father's weapons, a helmet, armour and shield, all gifts from Hephaestos at the glittering wedding of the king with the goddess. In addition Peleus gave him a javelin, a gift from Cheiron, which was so heavy that only Achilles could lift it, and also his divine horses, Xanthos and Balios, gifts of Poseidon. His inseparable comrade during the war was Patroklos, his childhood friend

Achilles tends the wound of his friend, Patroklos.

and son of Menoitios of Lokris, and also close to him was Phoinikas, son of Amyntor, who took the role of adviser and teacher.

Patroklos, who grew up with Achilles, was

115

by no means second to him in valour or in benevolence. Their close relationship is represented in particular on the inside of a kylix cup dating from 500 B.C., which shows with how much care Achilles, who had a good knowledge of medicine, tends the wound of his friend. Although in the first years of the war Patroklos did not take part in the battles, the Trojans who suffered demise at his hands later on were not few in number. He killed Sarpedon, the son of Zeus, but when his own time came, he was first hit by Apollo, and finally struck down by Hektor.

The part played by the other Achaeans was also very important: for instance there was Diomedes, son of Tydeus who was a fighter with outstanding morals and strength, Idomeneus and Meriones from Crete, the physicians and sons of Asklepios Podaleirios and Machaon, Tlepolemos son of Herakles, Akamas and Demophon, the sons of Theseus, and many others.

The Trojans

Priam, son of Laomedon and king of Troy, rebuilt the city again after the destruction wrought by Herakles. Together with Hekabe he produced nineteen sons, and thirty-one with other wives; he also produced twelve daughters. During the years of the Trojan War, he was an old man who, according to Homer, was remarkable for his nobleness and his leadership.

Hektor was the eldest son of Priam and it was he who, with a deep sense of responsibility, undertook to command the Trojan army. Brave and fearless, he wrought havoc among the enemy until the moment when Achilles came onto the battlefield and he finally found death at his hands. With Andromache, daughter of Eëtion, he had a son, Astyanax.

Even before his birth it was known that **Paris**, who abducted Helen and caused the war, would bring great destruction to the city. When she bore him, Hekabe dreamed that she had given birth to a flaming torch which dripped blood and set fire to Troy. This was why the royal couple decided to kill the new-born baby and ordered a shepherd to expose him on Mount Ida. The compassion felt

by the shepherd kept Paris alive and later on he was acknowledged as the true son of his father.

Tragic **Cassandra**, the very beautiful daughter of Priam, was loved by Apollo who in order to possess her

promised to teach her the art of prophecy. When she did not keep her own promise to him, Apollo placed a curse on her that her prophecies would never be believed by mortals.

Aeneas, the most important of the warriors in the Trojan camp after Hektor, was the son of Aphrodite and her favourite. He was injured in his duel with Diomedes and it was his mother who saved him, together with Apollo. When he came face to face with Achilles Poseidon saved him, so that he could later on succeed Priam.

Sarpedon, king of Lycia, had gone to Troy to help Priam. He was the son of Zeus and Europa and the brother of Minos and Rhadamanthos. Some believed that he was the son of Zeus and

Laodameia, daughter of Bellerophon. Although he was the son of a god, he lost his life through a javelin thrown by Patroklos. On the orders of Zeus, Hypnos and Thanatos undertook to convey his corpse back to far-off Lycia.

The tenth year of the war and the fall of Troy

After the Achaeans had fought for ten years without success, a quite unrelated event changed the course of developments. Chryse, a priest of Apollo and father of the beautiful and clever Chryseis who had been taken prisoner and handed to Agamemnon, came to the Greek camp. When he asked Agamemnon to return his daughter to him the king refused, and only changed his mind when Apollo showed his anger. He put as a condition, however, that Achilles should give him his own slave-girl, Briseis. The two kings had a fierce altercation and finally Achilles withdrew and in anger decided that he would not participate in the fighting again. A little later fierce skirmishes broke out between the two armies. On the first day of battle Diomedes excelled himself and on the following day Hektor fought with Ajax the Telamonian, but without result. Hektor's onslaught was so great that it seemed nothing would be able to stop him. Agitated, Agamemnon suggested that they abandon the siege, but his idea was rejected. Instead, the Achaeans decided to send representatives to persuade Achilles to return to the battlefield. Achilles refused and the third day saw an Agamemnon who was

The embassy sent by the Achaeans to Achilles consisted of Phoinikas, Odysseus, and Ajax; the latter is missing here and another young man, perhaps Patroklos, is depicted in his place.

The Greeks had difficulty in recovering the body of the dead Patroklos whose weapons Hektor had already stolen. When they brought him back to their camp, they organized athletic contests to honour his memory.

Thetis went to Hephaestos and asked him to fashion new armour for her only son. The god made a helmet, a breastplate, greaves, and a shield which depicted lands, the oceans, the sky, the sun, the moon and the stars. The very next morning Thetis presented her son with his new weapons.

Myrmidons. Achilles consented and gave him his weapons to use. Seeing him, the Trojans thought he was Achilles and turned to flee. Patroklos in his ardour believed that he could now capture Troy; however Apollo wounded him and then Hektor found an opportunity to

Agamemnon returned Briseis to him. However, he asked Thetis to bring him new weapons so that he could rush back into the battle. All prepared, Achilles, in spite of the warning from his mother that if he were to kill Hektor he would lose his own life, plunged into battle. Butchering like a madman, he put the Trojans to flight. Even Hektor, who had remained

"The Triumph of Achilles", Achilleion, Kerkyra (Corfu).

very effective on the battlefield, although he was wounded and had to retire. Since the Trojans were now desperately trying to get near to the Greek camp, Patroklos asked Achilles to allow him to enter the fight leading his

kill him. Achilles went into mourning immediately on hearing of the loss of his friend and decided to get his revenge. His fellow warriors tried to soothe his pain and

to the last, turned to run. Achilles however, whom nobody could outpace, went after him and caught him. After killing him with his javelin, blinded by rage, he stripped him, bound him behind his

*As the leader of the forces of Troy had been killed, **Penthesileia**, queen of the Amazons and daughter of Ares, arrived in Troy to render assistance. Fearlessly she threw herself into the battle, killed many Achaeans and did not hesitate to face even Achilles himself. When he pierces her with his spear she, the haughty one, looks at him with an expression of the passion that had developed between them. Achilles does not leave her dead, but carries her off the battlefield so that she will not be defiled.*

*The body of Hektor remained on the ground beside the Achaean camp, until **Priam** himself came to ask for it with gifts and ransom. **Achilles** handed over the body to the devastated father and suggested that the war be suspended until the funeral of Hektor had taken place.*

chariot and dragged him to the Achaean camp.

When Achilles had killed Hektor, Penthesileia, and Memnon his own hour approached, as Thetis had warned. Having put the Trojans to flight, shortly before he set foot in the citadel of Troy, Apollo gave Paris an order to aim at the only vulnerable part of his body, his heel; his instant death was the result. Ajax the Telamonian managed to retrieve the corpse of the dead Achilles from the hands of the enemy and bring it back to the Achaean camp. The grieving Achaeans, Thetis and the Nereids mourned for him for seventeen whole days and nights. Then they burned him on a pyre and buried him next to Patroklos, organizing funeral games in his honour. Having decided on the capture of Troy, the Greeks called a general assembly to plan it. The seer Calchas revealed to the gathering that Helenos, son of Priam, was the only one who knew of the conditions under which his

*When Thetis decided to present the arms of her dead son to the Achaeans, they were claimed by both Odysseus and Ajax. The wise Nestor, in order to avoid a dispute, asked the Trojans to decide who was worthy to have them. When the arms were given to Odysseus, **Ajax**, mortally offended, rammed his sword into the ground, fell on it and killed himself.*

Ajax the Telamonian brings the dead Achilles to the Achaean camp.

*From the blood of Ajax, who killed himself, there sprang up **Consolida ajacis**, a flower which took the name of the hero and bears the initials AI on its petals.*

The bow and arrows of Herakles were in the possession of **Philoktetes**, whom the Achaeans had abandoned on Lemnos after he had been bitten by a snake there on the journey to Troy. Odysseus, accompanied by Diomedes, found him still there - ten years later - and having taken the weapons from him, they forced him to go with them.

Odysseus found Neoptolemos, son of Achilles and Deidameia, in the palace of his grandfather on Skyros. After handing him his father's weapons, they persuaded him without difficulty to accompany them to Troy.

Odysseus stole the palladion from the temple of Athena one night with the help of Diomedes. Helen helped Odysseus in this difficult task when he entered the city in disguise and she showed him exactly where it was to be found.

city could be taken. Therefore Odysseus took Helenos prisoner, and from him they learned that the prerequisites which had to be met in order to achieve their goal were for them to have the bow and arrows of Herakles, for Neoptolemos son of Achilles to fight, and for them

to steal the palladion, the sacred wooden statue of Athena, from Troy. All of these tasks were undertaken and carried out by Odysseus, aided by Diomedes. When he had fulfilled

the prerequisites stated by Helenos for the capture of Troy, Odysseus – on the advice of Athena – devised a plan based on the famous 'Trojan Horse'. To be exact, he entrusted to the carpenter Epeios from Phocis the task of

According to one account, Odysseus took the arms of Achilles after lots were drawn.

The carpenter
Epeios built the Trojan Horse
with the support and assistance
of Athena.

constructing a huge wooden horse with hidden openings in its enormous belly. When the horse was ready, he selected his bravest fighters and they hid in the belly. The rest, led by Agamemnon, boarded the ships and sailed away from the harbour, under the pretence that they were abandoning the war. Only Sinon remained in the camp; it was his job to set the plan into motion. As soon as the Trojans woke up next morning they found the enemy camp deserted and the strange construction, the Trojan Horse, in front of the walls. Full of questions, they began to seek an explanation. When they discovered Sinon, who pretended to be hiding, they began an interrogation. Sinon, who had been well instructed, said that the Achaeans had left because Calchas had revealed that Athena

The "Trojan Horse", Giovanni Domenico Tiepolo, 1773, National Gallery, London.

was very angry with them for having stolen the palladion. The seer had instructed them to take it back to Greece immediately and in its place to leave the horse as an offering for her temple. In order to justify his own presence there he said that he had escaped

Athena, who instilled in Odysseus the idea of the Trojan Horse, wonders at the perfect construction.

from the Achaeans who had wanted to sacrifice him in order to gain a favourable wind so that the ships could sail. The Trojans believed Sinon and full of joy, despite the objections of Cassandra and Laocoon, they took the horse into the city. As soon as night fell, Sinon signalled to the Greeks in the ships with a blazing torch to come back, and at the same time the heroes spilled out of the belly of the horse, in order to open the city gates to them. Thus the Achaeans entered Troy and unhindered, began to slaughter and pillage. Neoptolemos killed Priam and threw Astyanax, son of Hektor, from the walls. The only one saved from catastrophe was Aeneas, because the Greeks knew that he was under the protection of Zeus. At the same time Menelaos seized Helen and they all went back victorious to the ships, having taken priceless booty and many Trojan women as slaves. Among the latter was Andromache, who was taken by Neoptolemos, and Cassandra who left along with Agamemnon. After ten years of war, the Achaeans set sail for their homeland.

Laocoon, brother of Anchises and a seer and priest of Apollo, tried in vain to persuade the Trojans of the evil that the Trojan Horse concealed. When subsequently two snakes came from the sea and devoured him and his son, everyone believed that he had been punished for his imprudent prophecies. Laocoon and his sons. 1st cent. A.D. Vatican Museum.

*Among the acts of violence and pillaging which the Achaeans carried out during the sack of Troy was the **rape of Cassandra**, daughter of Priam, by Ajax the Locrian, at the very moment when she supplicated herself before the statue of Athena. For this impious deed Ajax was punished by Athena, who sank his ship and drowned him on his way home.*

The return of the heroes

The Achaeans had carried out many barbarous acts during the sack of Troy; except for Nestor, Diomedes, Neoptolemos and Idomeneus, all roamed for a number of years before they were able to return home.

Menelaos had a smooth journey, after one stop at Sounion where he buried his captain, Phrontes, who died suddenly; nevertheless when heading south, a strong wind blew him to Egypt. After seven years of wandering in unknown parts he decided to return home. However, he forgot to make sacrifices to the gods and thus departure was impossible. At length, with the help of Eidothea, daughter of Proteus, he was able to trap that old man of the sea in order to learn what he had to do to be able to go home. The latter advised him to return to Egypt and sacrifice to Zeus on the banks of the Nile. This he did, and Menelaos and Helen were able to see Sparta again after eight years of wanderings.

Agamemnon, who had left separately from his brother, met with a great tempest off Kapherea in

Tragic Cassandra shared the same fate as Agamemnon, who had brought her as a slave from Troy. Mercilessly, Clytemnestra killed her, raising the axe in her own hands.

The unscrupulous Aegisthos killed Agamemnon, despite the pleas of Elektra.

124

Orestes kills the awful Aegisthos, the murderer of his father.

Euboia, and lost many ships. When he finally arrived at Mycenae great misfortune awaited him. Unsuspecting, he was murdered by his own wife, Clytemnestra, who had formed a relationship with Aegisthos, the son of Thyestes. The latter actually carried out the slaying of Agamemnon, and then ruled with Clytemnestra in Argos and Mycenae where, eight years later the young son of Agamemnon, Orestes, made his appearance. The youth had grown up in Phocis, where his mother had sent him; now he arrived with his friend Pylades, intending to avenge the loss of his father. He met with his sister Elektra and with her help killed his mother and her lover. As this was matricide the Furies, goddesses of remorse, began to pursue him. He fled to Athens and with the help of Athena gained his acquittal by the Areopagos. Even though Athena herself took on the Furies and transformed them into the Eumenides, some of them escaped and continued to pursue him. After his misfortunes Orestes sought the help of Apollo who advised him to bring to Attica the wooden statue of Artemis, which was in the land of the Taurans. He was taken prisoner in far-off Scythia, where he went with his companion, Pylades, and led to the temple of Artemis to be sacrificed. There however he found his sister, Iphigeneia, and after they recognized each other they managed to flee together, having stolen the wooden statue of the goddess. After this success, he built a temple to honour Artemis in Vravrona in Attica, and finally managed to regain the throne of his father.

Orestes and the Furies, Adolphe-William Bouguereau, 1862.

125

THE ODYSSEY

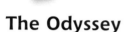

The Odyssey

Apart from Menelaos and the other heroes who suffered on their return to their homeland from Troy, the one who met with the greatest adventures on the journey home was Odysseus. His ten-year, mythical adventure on the way from Troy to Ithaca is related by Homer in his second epic poem, the Odyssey. Cleverness, ingenuity, courage but above all, endurance – these were the characteristics of the precious 'comrades' of the hero on his turbulent 'odyssey'. Starting from real locations, such as the land of the Cicones, he was to pass through a series of fantastic places - attempts have been made in vain to locate them on the map - to reach his kingdom of Ithaca where his faithful wife Penelope and his son Telemachos had waited for him for twenty years.

In the land of the Cicones

When Odysseus and his comrades left Troy, a strong wind blew them northwards and forced them to stop in Ismaros in Thrace, a place inhabited by the Cicones somewhere between the rivers Evros and Nestos. Given that this was a folk which, during the Trojan War had taken the opposing side, Odysseus had no compunction about going ashore and plundering the district. However, when his friends arranged a feast in his honour, the people from the hinterland came up and attacked them. After a battle lasting a whole day Odysseus was obliged to depart, having lost twenty men.

In the land of the Lotus-eaters

Leaving the Cicones, Odysseus headed south. However, the winds that he met off Cape Malea changed his course and after ten days he arrived in the land of the Lotus-eaters. They took their name from the 'lotus', a fruit or the flower of a fruit which caused whoever consumed it to lose his memory. They themselves ate the lotus and whenever strangers arrived they would extend to them

The only one who escaped the terrible devastation was **Maro**, a priest of Apollo. Odysseus spared him, and he reciprocated by showering him with gifts – wine, gold and silver.

Odysseus and his comrades blind Polyphemos

peaceable hospitality and offer them this fruit of forgetfulness. Whosoever made the mistake of tasting the fruit forgot his homeland and his family and stayed there. Three of the comrades tried the magic fruit, so that Odysseus was obliged to bind them fast in order to take them away with him. After the land of the Lotus-eaters, Odysseus arrived in the land of the Cyclopes, giants who had only one eye in their forehead. They were fierce, lived in caves, and were only concerned with the pasturing of their flocks. After resting for a day, on the morrow Odysseus decided to explore the terrain. He took a skin filled with the wine that Maro of the Cicones had given him, and along with twelve comrades set out in the unknown countryside. They went into the first cave they came across, beside the sea, ate meat and cheese and waited to meet the inhabitant. Enormous Polyphemos, son of Poseidon and Thoosa, arrived just before nightfall. He put the animals inside the cave, closed it off, milked them and sat down to rest. The Achaeans, were terrified and hid, and even though Odysseus presented himself to the Cyclops and tried to explain how they came to be there, Polyphemos seized two of the comrades and devoured them. Next morning he ate two more, closed off the entrance and went away. On his return in the evening, when he had eaten another two, Odysseus offered him wine and made him drunk. Immediately wily Odysseus, who had fashioned a huge branch into a point, thrust it into the fire, lifted it with the help of the comrades and

Odysseus escapes from the cave of Polyphemus. Theodor van Thulden (1606-1669), Museum of Fine Arts, San Francisco.

Bound beneath the belly of a ram, Odysseus escapes from the Cyclops.

blinded the Cyclops with it. Wailing in pain, Polyphemos asked who had done this, to which Odysseus replied 'nobody'. The next day, blinded, he opened the entrance and when the animals went out he felt their backs one by one in order to catch the strangers. However, clever Odysseus had told them to bind themselves beneath the bellies of the rams, and thus they managed to escape.

On the island of Aeolos

Leaving the fierce Cyclopes behind him, Odysseus arrived on the island of Aeolos, lord of the winds. Aeolos and his wife gave hospitality to the Achaean fleet for a whole month, and when they decided to leave handed them a flask in which all the winds had been imprisoned except for the benevolent Zephyros. They warned them not to open it until they had arrived at their destination. Thus, after a very pleasant journey of ten days, Odysseus drew near to Ithaca. Tired as he was, he went to sleep and his friends in their curiosity opened the flask. A storm blew up which took them back to the island of Aeolos. As the latter refused to help them again, they resumed their journey of adventure.

In the land of the Laestrygones

Seven days after leaving the island of Aeolos, Odysseus' ships arrived in an unknown place. He sent three comrades to find out where they were. When they went to the palace of Antiphates and encountered the queen, they were terrified because she was enormous, a real giant. The king was similar in appearance and immediately on his arrival he devoured one of the three. The other two ran off in flight but the army of the giants pursued them and when they arrived in the harbour they threw rocks and destroyed all the Achaean ships. Only Odysseus, who had anchored further out, managed to save his ship and the forty-five comrades who accompanied him.

Wright Barker, 1900

On the island of Circe

The ship of Odysseus continued on its journey to Aeaea, the island of Circe who was the daughter of Helios and the sister of Aeëtes, king of Colchis.

Odysseus in Hades

Circe prepares the magic potion for Odysseus, while one of the metamorphosed comrades looks on.

At dawn on the following day, they left Circe and went on to the land of the Cimmerians at the ends of the Ocean. Odysseus and two of his comrades followed the instructions of Circe and arrived at the entrance to Hades where he made sacrifices and prayed to Hades and Persephone. After facing the souls he met with, who were thirsting for the blood of the sacrifices, he came to Teiresias. The seer revealed to him that, as he had blinded Polyphemos, he had provoked the anger of Poseidon who had placed obstacles along his journey. He went on to tell him that if they molested the cattle and sheep of Helios in Thrinakia, they would experience more difficulty before they returned. In that case he would arrive alone and on a foreign ship at Ithaca, where he would find dozens of suitors claiming his wife. Thus spoke Teiresias and went away. Leaving the souls to drink the blood of the sacrifices, Odysseus met the spirit of his mother Antikleia who told him

In order to establish who would go and explore, they drew lots and thus Eurylochos went off with half of the comrades. When they arrived at the palace they were welcomed by Circe; she gave them a drink which made them forget everything and then with her magic wand she transformed them into swine. Eurylochos, who had not gone into the palace himself, realized that something awful had happened and returned to Odysseus. Just as he decided to go himself, Hermes appeared and gave him an antidote which would neutralize Circe's magic. The witch, when she saw that her spells failed, promised Odysseus that she would change the comrades back into men if he would lay with her. After a year of gracious living on the island, Odysseus and the comrades decided to leave. Circe counselled him to go to Hades and find the seer Teiresias, so that he would give him instructions as to how to return to his homeland.

Odysseus, with his two comrades, listens carefully to the prophecies of the seer Teiresias, gazing at his head which is located near his feet.

what was happening in his homeland. After meeting many more spirits, mainly those of women of heroic families, he came upon Agamemnon, who related to him what had happened on his return to Mycenae, and Achilles who wanted to hear of the heroic deeds of his son Neoptolemos during the sack of Troy. Angry because of the affair concerning the arms of Achilles, Ajax did not want to talk to his opponent Odysseus, despite the endeavours of the latter. Finally, he saw Minos, Tityos, Tantalos, Sisyphos and Herakles but then took to his heels when he was surrounded by countless souls of the dead, all demanding to drink blood.

comrades returned to the island of Circe, to bury dead Elpenor whose soul they had met in the Underworld. Next morning, they left for the island of the fiendish Sirens who, with their bewitching melodies, enchanted passers-by and then kept them there

The island of the Sirens

Putting awful Hades behind them, Odysseus and the

forever. They would be so intoxicated by their songs that they lost all interest in food and drink, until they finally perished. Following instructions

Coin from Akragas, Sicily, c. 420-410 B.C.

from Circe, Odysseus stopped the ears of his comrades with wax, while he himself – not wishing to miss the experience but not wanting to endanger himself – ordered them to bind him hand and foot to the mast of the ship. Indeed, when he heard the bewitching songs of the Sirens, he could not resist. To his good fortune though, when he begged his comrades to release him they could not hear him, and thus they managed to pass this danger without any losses.

The passage between Scylla and Charybdis

After passing by the terrible Sirens, they had to pass through the narrow strait between Scylla and Charybdis. Alternatively, they could have passed between the Clashing Rocks – moving cliffs from which only the

Argo had escaped, but they preferred to follow the advice of Circe who suggested that they pass by Scylla. The latter, which lived on a cliff, was a terrible monster with twelve legs, six heads and three rows of teeth; every time a ship passed she would stretch out her necks and seize the sailors. Opposite her was the rock of Charybdis which, three times daily, sucked up the water from the sea and then spewed it out, creating huge waves. Odysseus, who had been told by Circe that it would be better to lose six of his comrades than all of them, chose to pass close to the rock of Scylla. Then, while all in terror watched Charybdis suck in and spew out the waters of the sea, Scylla struck and seized six of the comrades and devoured them alive. Horrified, the survivors rowed quickly until they arrived at the island of Thrinakia.

The island of Thrinakia

Drawing near to the island, Odysseus remembered the words of Teiresias, according to which he was not to lay hands on any of the sacred animals of Helios. He decided not to stop there and thus avoid temptation. His comrades, however, were exhausted from the journey, and asked to rest, swearing that they would not touch the animals. So they went ashore, ate, drank, mourned their lost comrades and fell asleep. The bad weather which began on the following day kept them on the island for a whole month. Despairing, Odysseus saw that they had exhausted their food supplies, and went to ask for help from the gods. However, sleep overcame him and then the comrades decided to slaughter some cows and sacrifice a portion of them to Helios. This had hardly happened when the latter asked Zeus to punish them. When, after six days had passed the Achaeans, sated and rested, decided to leave, Zeus sent his thunder and lightning. The boat was destroyed and all were lost at sea, except for Odysseus who had not tasted the flesh of the divine cattle.

Odysseus and Kalypso. Max Beckmann, 1943, Kunsthalle, Hamburg.

On the island of Calypso

All alone, with only a mast and a keel bound with rope to float on, Odysseus was tossed around by the sea for nine days and nine nights, until the gods cast him up on Ogygia. On this distant and beautiful island there lived the nymph Calypso, daughter of Atlas. This beautiful nymph welcomed the shipwrecked Odysseus, took care of him and gave herself totally to him. When after a short while Odysseus wanted to leave, Calypso, who had fallen in love with him in the meantime, tried to detain him by every means. Not being able to do otherwise, since he had no ship and no comrades, Odysseus stayed with her for seven whole years. He would indeed have remained there for the rest of his life, if Athena had not had a hand in it. The goddess went to Zeus and complained because he had left Odysseus to suffer for so many years. As the other gods agreed, and Poseidon was away in Ethiopia, Zeus sent Hermes to demand that Calyso set Odysseus free. Even though she was not at all pleased by the suggestion of Hermes, she was obliged to comply so as not to come into conflict with the gods. She therefore promised that she would help him to make a raft so that he could go by sea. Finally, when after four months the raft was ready, the nymph loaded it with provisions and sent Odysseus with a favourable wind to the island of the Phaeacians.

The island of the Phaeacians

After a journey of eighteen days Odysseus began to make out land and would have

The meeting of Odysseus with Nausicaa

arrived in Scheria within a short time if Poseidon had not noticed him as he was returning from Ethiopia. Because he had not forgiven him for killing his son Polyphemos, he sent him new tribulations. He stirred up the sea with his trident, broke up the raft, and Odysseus found himself floundering again for three whole days in an unknown sea. Thankfully Leukothea, a sea deity, arrived and helped him set foot finally on Scheria, where the Phaeacians lived under their king, Alkinoos. His wife Arete was also his niece, and they had one daughter, Nausicaa, and five sons. The first person whom Odysseus met when he woke up on the shore of the island, was the king's daughter herself who had come down to the river to wash clothes, following instructions from Athena who had appeared to her in a dream. Calm and affable, she took care of Odysseus who asked her for help. She gave him clothes and food and then showed him the way to the palace. Finally, she advised him to ignore everyone, including the king, and throw

Odysseus and Nausicaa, 1619, Alte Pinakothek, Munich.

himself at the feet of queen Arete, seeking help. So Odysseus went as a supplicant to the palace and moved the royal couple not only to help him but also do him honour by organizing athletic contests and feasts. At the fairwell dinner, when the bard Demodokos sang of the Trojan Horse, Odysseus was moved to tears. Then the king, although he was of a very discreet nature, asked him who he was. He answered that he was Odysseus, son of Laertes, and gave an account of his adventures. The Phaeacians were proud that they had given hospitality to such a great hero and on the following day they presented him with rich gifts and a ship to take him back to Ithaca.

The return of Odysseus, Bernardino di Benedetto, 1509, National Gallery, London.

Odysseus in Ithaca

The Phaeacian ship brought Odysseus to Ithaca. As he had been asleep for the whole of the journey, when they arrived they left him on the seashore with all his gifts and set off for the return voyage.

In the meantime, however, all on Ithaca believed that Odysseus was dead. Thus his father Laertes, a widower and unhappy because he believed that he had lost his son, had withdrawn to an estate far from the rest of the world. In the palace, however, a dramatic state of affairs had developed. Suitors had gathered from Ithaca and all the islands around to claim Penelope as a wife. She however, believing in Odysseus, tricked them by saying that they should first allow her to weave a shroud for Laertes. However, to gain time, she wove by day but unravelled the weaving by night. This went on for three years, until a slave betrayed her to the suitors who were furious and caught her in the act. Thereafter they assembled in the palace every day and amused themselves by tearing apart the

For three whole years Penelope wove the same garment, deceiving the suitors

Odysseus avidly shoots down the suitors

property of her son, Telemachos. The latter, although twenty years old, had not yet taken any initiative until at the instigation of Athena he made an attempt to chase out the suitors. After he failed he travelled to Pylos, hoping perhaps to learn something of his father through Nestor. The moment Odysseus awoke on the seashore where the Phaeacians had left him, Athena appeared and after telling him about the situation that prevailed on Ithaca, she transformed him into a beggar and sent him to find the swineherd, Eumaios. Soon, Athena contrived that Telemachos also arrived there; he recognized his father and immediately they began to plan how to destroy the suitors.

Odysseus, as a beggar, arrived at the palace. After a moving scene of recognition with his dog Argos and after he had appeared before Penelope and reassured her that her husband lived, there followed his recognition by the old nurse Eurykleia. That same day Penelope had taken a decision: she would announce to the suitors that she would marry the one who managed to bend the great bow of Odysseus, string it, and then shoot an arrow through twelve axes placed in a row. So it happened. The next day all the suitors assembled, strewed the tables and began to torment the beggar who, at the queen's orders, was seated next to Telemachos. Shortly, Penelope appeared

and announced what form the contest would take. All tried but nobody managed to succeed, and when Odysseus asked to compete, they finally consented to let him do so despite all objections. Without any difficulty, he shot through the axes and immediately, helped by Telemachos and Eumaios, began a mad attack on the suitors. Penelope however, continued to disbelieve that her husband had arrived and only when the two were alone together was he able to persuade her by revealing some shared secret. Then, in tears, she fell into his arms and his trials had finally come to an end.

Index

Bibliography

Baumann, H., *Die griechische Pflanzenwelt in Mythos, Kunst und Literatur* (1982).

Bérard, C., *A City of Images: Iconography and Society in Ancient Greece* (1989).

Bell, R.E., *Dictionary of Classical Mythology* (1982).

Birchall, A., & Corbett, P.E., *Greek Gods and Heroes* (1974).

Burkert, W., *Greek Religion* (1985).

Carpenter, T.H., *Art and Myth in Ancient Greece* (1991).

Carpenter, T.H., *Dionysian Imagery* (1986).

Finley, M. I., *The world of Odysseus* (1967).

Graves, Robert. *The Greek Myths* (1981).

Grimal, P. *Dictionary of Classical Mythology* (1986).

Κακριδής, Ι.Θ., κ.α., *Ελληνική Μυθολογία*, 1-5 (1986).

Κερένυϊ. Κ. *Η μυθολογία των Ελλήνων* (1974).

Lexicon Iconographicum Mythologiae Classicae, Zurich 1981-1988.

Nilsson, M. P. *Geschichte der Griechischen Religion* (1955).

Παπαχατζής, Ν.Δ., *Η θρησκεία στην αρχαία Ελλάδα* (1987).

Σέρβη Κ., *Ελληνική Μυθολογία* (1996).

Shapiro, H.A., *Myth into Art* (1994).

Shapiro, A., *Art and Cult under the Tyrants in Athens* (1989).

Simon, E., *Die Göter der Griechen*, München 1980.

Trendall, A.D. and Webster, T.B.L., *Illustrations of Greek Drama* (1971).

Ψιλάκης Ν. *Κρητική Μυθολογία* (1996).

All of the sketches are of representations on ancient Greek vases which are on display in various museums all over the world and have appeared in numerous publications.